Samson Revisited

Samson Revisited

A study of Judges 13-16: in defence of Samson as a man of faith

Michael Storey

"One man of you shall chase a thousand: for the LORD your God, he it is that fighteth for you, as he hath promised you. Take good heed therefore unto yourselves, that ye love the LORD your God." (Joshua 23:10,11)

The Christadelphian

404 Shaftmoor Lane, Hall Green, Birmingham B28 8SZ, UK

2017

First published 2017

ISBN 978 0 85189 392 1 (print edition)
ISBN 978 0 85189 393 8 (electronic edition)

Printed and bound in the UK by
Short Run Press Limited

Contents

Preface

THE following chapters are the result of an on / off personal study of the record of Samson over the past few years. This was triggered by a request to speak about him to a group of young people, and an acknowledgement that after fifty years in the Truth, my own understanding of Samson, and his role in the purpose of God, was not clear. I respected the views of him I had read and heard presented by others, but was uncomfortable with the usual interpretation of the record of the strong man of Israel.

Samson is usually portrayed as a wayward, lustful man; a man who failed in keeping his vow as a Nazarite, and yet somehow was listed in the epistle to the Hebrews chapter 11 as an example of faith – one who received a good report through faith. But this view of Samson raised a number of questions in my mind that I needed answering. And so the decision was made that the time had come to *revisit* the inspired record of Samson, and to see if I could finally decide for myself what kind of man the inspired scriptures portrayed him to be, and what lessons I could learn from the record of his life.

These studies of Samson are not though, in any way, intended to be exhaustive. There are still unanswered questions that need to be addressed. However, the result of the many hours of study I have engaged in is presented humbly in the following pages and with all sincerity. Some of my thoughts regarding

Samson as a man of faith I am aware are held by others who also do not believe him to be the flawed hero usually presented. They, however, may have come to different conclusions regarding parts of the narrative from those I put forward in these studies.

These thoughts on the record of Samson are also set forth with the realisation that for others to accept them, especially those who sincerely hold a different view of Samson from the one presented in these pages, they will have to do as I set out to do, and empty their mind of all preconceived ideas of the man who was given by God as a saviour for His people. This, for some, may not be possible as I realise it means questioning the usual interpretation of the scripture record concerning him and seeing if what has been recorded could be viewed from a different standpoint, but always in line with the rest of scripture. The following studies are therefore set forth without the desire to be controversial or dogmatic, even though we shall question from time to time the usual interpretation of the events recorded and suggest we can view them from another angle, and so come to different conclusions.

For me the result of these studies is that the difficulties I have had with the record of Samson for many years have all but disappeared. I now truly believe Israel's God-given saviour was a man of faith, as the epistle to the Hebrews presents him; a man through whom God worked, but who like all men and women felt the frailties of the flesh and did sin; a man who in the things recorded of him was nevertheless, in many ways, a type of the Lord Jesus Christ – *the Saviour* – who did not sin and who was given for our salvation. Equally I believe he is a man whose 'life' has many vital lessons that are written for our learning, lessons which we shall consider as our studies unfold. The types and ways in which Samson portrays the life and work of the Master will be left, in the main, until the final chapter. However, some will be obvious from the narrative as we seek to expound it.

If these studies do nothing more than help and encourage readers to look again prayerfully at the record of Samson in God's revealed word, as I set out to do, and to gain exhortation for their walk to the kingdom, then they have served their purpose.

Michael Storey
Coventry, July 2017

Abbreviations:

- KJV – King James Version
- Strong – Strong's Exhaustive Concordance of the Bible
- BDB – Brown-Driver-Briggs – a Hebrew and English Lexicon of the Old Testament
- Rotherham's – The Emphasised Bible – J. B. Rotherham
- TWOT – Theological Wordbook of the Old Testament
- YLT – Young's Literal Translation of the Bible
- NET Bible – New English Translation
- ESV – English Standard Version

Note: When in the studies reference is made to the Hebrew or Greek word and its definition, these are taken from Strong's Hebrew and Greek Dictionaries unless otherwise stated.

1 |

The background to Samson

Man of faith or failure?

M OST commentators, it would seem, see Samson, the last of the saviours God raised up, as typical of the children of Israel at the time of the Judges. He is portrayed as someone who did that which was right in his own eyes. He is presented as an enigma; a puzzle. His life is portrayed as that of a wayward warrior who lusts after Philistine women and pays the penalty, a man who played with fire and in the end got burnt.

He is described as a deeply flawed hero whose life was unduly entangled with the Philistines against whom he fought. He is said to have violated a number of the Ten Commandments, as well as his Nazarite vow, and to have exhibited in his own tragic-heroic life the traits of the people of Israel during that period of their history. While he was used by God for deliverance, and while he even called upon God on occasions to help him, his life was nevertheless one of continual unfaithfulness – just like the nation he judged.

Yet despite all that, and the fact that there is no record of him repenting or asking God for forgiveness, he manages to be included in the list of the faithful in the epistle to the Hebrews chapter 11!

Is this the picture of Samson that the Almighty wishes us to see? If it is, then Samson has many negative lessons to teach us. But is that really what God intends us to learn from him, or can we look at the record of Samson in a different way? If we regard him as the kind of man we have described, are we misjudging the last of the judges recorded in the book of Judges? The present writer believes we are.

The following studies, therefore, seek to redress the balance concerning Samson. To do this means putting aside any preconceived ideas about him and revisiting the scripture record of his life. We have to humbly, and prayerfully, compare scripture with scripture in order to discover what the Lord reveals concerning His purpose with him. We may not be able to answer all the questions regarding the record of his 'life' but we believe we can defend Samson as a man of faith who did sin, but who, for the majority of his life as recorded in the inspired record, is also a type of our Lord Jesus Christ. In addition, he is a man who provides many positive, as well as some negative, lessons that we can take to ourselves, besides those that his faithful, God-driven actions should have taught the people of his day.

The time period of Samson's life
To understand God's purpose with Samson, and his faith in the Lord, we first need to look at the time period in which he lived. As the days of the Judges came towards an end, God once more found it necessary to chasten His chosen people because they did evil in His sight (Judges 13:1). Time and again they had turned away from the worship of Yahweh their God and worshipped the gods of the nations they should have destroyed, including the gods of the Philistines (Judges 10:6). However, unlike previous occasions when the Lord punished them, the people did not at this time cry unto Him. As the record of Samson will show us, they were quite content for the Philistines to have dominion over them. But the God of Israel is a God of compassion, mercy and grace. So even as the oppression by the Philistines for forty years commenced, and despite the fact that Israel did not this time call to Him for help, He Himself set in motion a plan that would

moderate their suffering and commence a process of deliverance. That plan centred on a child of promise to a barren woman; a child who from his birth was to be separated to God for the purpose of being a deliverer of his people; one who was to *begin* their deliverance from Philistine domination; a child who grew up to be rejected by those he came to save.

Each of the saviours God raised up in the days after the death of Joshua was unique. The way God delivered His people by these saviours followed a different pattern each time. Such was the case with Samson. For a start he was unique in that he was born to be a saviour, not chosen and raised up by God during his lifetime as were all the others. But Samson was to be unique in many other ways as our studies will reveal.

Samson was born into a family of the tribe of Dan. The Danites are mentioned in the first chapter of Judges as struggling to obtain the portion of the land allotted to them (Judges 1:34,35) as did the other tribes. They all failed fully to keep God's commandments concerning the people of the land and as a result faced the consequences which the Lord brought upon them.

"And the Amorites forced the children of Dan into the mountain: for they would not suffer them to come down to the valley."   (Judges 1:34)

The tribe of Dan also figures in events recorded in the last chapters of Judges. Chapters 17-21 form appendices to the book as does the book of Ruth. It appears these chapters cover events that took place in the early period of the Judges when it is emphasised, "In those days there was no king in Israel, but every man did that which was right in his own eyes".[1]

Judges 18 records that a portion of the tribe of Dan migrated north and re-established itself there. It seems these men and women from the tribe of Dan sought the easy way out. They initially sent out five spies to find another portion of land to conquer and inhabit, in addition to the one apportioned to them.

---

1   Judges 17:6. See also 18:1; 19:1; 21:25.

Note that it specifically says they were from Zorah and Eshtaol, the very first two places allotted to the tribe by Joshua and Eleazar as recorded in Joshua 19:40,41. This action on the part of the inhabitants of Zorah and Eshtaol was another example of the faithlessness of the people of God at that time in their history. Travelling north the spies lodged for the night in mount Ephraim, in the house of Micah. There they found a Levite who Micah had established to be an apostate priest in his house, along with the false gods he had made. The five spies consulted with the Levite concerning their mission and according to his word presumed that the Lord was to be with them (Judges 18:5,6,10).

Having completed their spying mission they went back to their brethren in Zorah and Eshtaol and assured them they had found the ideal place in which to dwell in the north of the land. It's ironical that they encouraged their brethren with the words, "Be not slothful to go, and to enter to possess the land" (verse 9), when this was part of the very reason they had failed to conquer all of the portion of the land already allotted to them.

And so this section of the tribe of Dan mustered six hundred men, girt with weapons of war, to conquer the northern city of Laish in order to establish a new territory for their tribe, and yet were not prepared to use those same weapons of war, in faith, to conquer fully the territory already given to them by Joshua. Added to that, in their migration to the north, they were prepared to use force to take the false items of worship from the house of Micah, along with his priest, the young Levite, and so set up false worship in the new city of Dan. This worship was still in place when Samson and Samuel were born, a time when even in the Tabernacle at Shiloh the priesthood was being corrupted by the sons of Eli.[2]

These events recorded in the last chapters of Judges are a subject in themselves. The record of them leaves us with important warnings of where disobedience, faithlessness and apostasy will lead us. Once we step away from the Lord's

2   Judges 18:3; cf. also the early chapters of 1 Samuel.

commands we are on the slippery slope to spiritual and eternal death. These things have been written for our learning.

A faithful remnant

But in contrast to these events, and the faithless people from the tribe of Dan that migrated north, Samson's parents were part of the faithful remnant that still lived in the portion allotted to them by Joshua. As we have already pointed out, the first two names mentioned as part of the tribe's inheritance in the book of Joshua were Zorah and Eshtaol. Zorah[3] – the home of Manoah and his wife and where God manifests Himself through an angel and reveals His purpose with Samson – and Eshtaol, were the very places where the Spirit of the Lord began to move Samson in contrast to those of the tribe that had left. This intervention of Yahweh that set in motion the purpose of delivering His people from the Philistine domination of that time, was, we believe, to lead to Samson displaying, in contrast to his fellow Danites, wonderful examples of faith in the Lord who worked through him. As we shall also see in a later chapter, the men of Judah, during the work of Samson, were to show the same lack of faith in the Lord as displayed by Samson's fellow tribesmen.

The problem of chronology

We have to compare scripture with scripture to attempt to see just where Samson fits into the history of Israel at this time. There are differences of opinion regarding the chronology of the period of the Judges and the times of the kings that followed. No clear timetable of events has been accepted by all, even though attempts have been made to harmonise the scripture records. We cannot therefore be dogmatic as to where Samson fits into the Bible chronology, so the following comments are offered as only a suggestion. However, they do point out some interesting links between Samson and the Ark of God in the days of Eli

3   Zorah and Eshtaol were on the border of Dan and Judah, both tribes being prominent in the record concerning Samson.

and Samuel. When, therefore did the forty-year oppression of Judges 13:1 possibly take place? As we have already seen, the last chapters of the book of Judges – chapters 17-21 – took place early on in the period of the times of the judges, as also did the story of Ruth. This therefore places the record of Samson's life immediately before the record of Samuel's, in the early chapters of 1 Samuel. Both records make it clear that Israel, during that time, were under the domination of the Philistines. The Samson record tells us it ended after forty years, and the record in 1 Samuel 7 says that Israel overcame the Philistines with the encouragement of Samuel. Are these two records covering the same period of history? If so, it is very probable that the lives of Samson and Samuel ran side by side as the two charts try to depict.[4]

---

4   These suggestions have been made by others – e.g., *Samuel the Seer* by Michael Ashton [CMPA] and *Samson* by Richard E. Evans [Internet]. Compare also Dr. Constable's notes on Judges [Internet].

Forty years of Philistine oppression
(Judges 13:1)

Eli judges forty years
(1 Samuel 4:18)

Ark twenty years in
Kirjath-jearim (1 Samuel 7:2)

Defeat at Eben-ezer; Ark taken
and returned (1 Samuel 5,6)

Samuel born?
(1 Samuel 1:20)

Samuel's life

Samson born
(Judges 13:24)

Samson's life –
less than forty years

Samson judges twenty years
(Judges 15:20)

Samson dies before the forty years
of oppression end (Judges 16:30,31)

Victory at Mizpeh under Samuel. End of the forty
years of Philistine oppression (1 Samuel 7:13)

Possible chronology of Samson and Samuel

Eli and the Ark of God	Samuel	Samson
Eli and sons corrupt priesthood (1 Samuel 2,3).	Hannah prays for a son; Samuel promised (1 Samuel 1).	Philistine oppression of forty years begins because Israel did evil (Judges 13).
Prophecy that it would come to an end (1 Samuel 3).	Samuel born and given back to God (1 Samuel 1).	Samson's birth announced by angel (Judges 13).
Eli's sons die in battle with the Philistines and the Ark of God is taken (1 Samuel 4).	God appears to Samuel; prophecy about the end of Eli's house (1 Samuel 3).	To be one separated; he will *begin* to deliver Israel (Judges 13).
Following news that the Ark is taken Eli dies after judging for forty years (1 Samuel 4).	Grows up and God is with him; established as a prophet (1 Samuel 3).	Samson's birth; grows up and God blesses him and moves him (Judges 13:24,25).
The Ark is seven months in Philistine territory (1 Samuel 5,6).	After the death of Eli he judges Israel in Ramah (1 Samuel 7).	Samson's conflicts with the Philistines; judges Israel twenty years (Judges 14-16).
The Ark is returned (1 Samuel 6).	Samuel appeals to people (1 Samuel 7).	Death of Samson before forty years end (Judges 16).
The Ark is in Kirjath-Jearim for twenty years (1 Samuel 7).	Philistines subdued during Samuel's judgeship (1 Samuel 7).	Philistine oppression ends after forty years (1 Samuel 7).

If Samson and Samuel *were* born within a few years of each other, as we are suggesting, then Samson's conflicts with the Philistines seem best to fit the time period between Eli's death, immediately following the first battle of Eben-ezer (1 Samuel

4),[5] and the battle of 1 Samuel 7:10-13 some twenty years later. It was probably this same period of time when Samson judged Israel (see Judges 15:20). This puts Samson's judgeship of the people in between Eli's, and during some of the time of Samuel's.

It may have been the fall of Dagon's temple and the death of Samson (16:30), along with the abiding of the Ark of God in the house of Abinadab for twenty years, that inspired Israel's lamentation after the Lord and their revival under Samuel's leadership in 1 Samuel 7:3-9.

Had his example of faith finally been noted? Just as God had been with and helped Samson, so now when the people, encouraged by Samuel, turned to serve and trust God, He helped them to discomfort and smite the Philistines at Mizpeh. This brought an end to the forty years oppression and the work of delivering the people that Samson had begun. So a stone was erected signifying that 'Yahweh hath helped us' (1 Samuel 7:10-12).

Samson and the Ark of God

There are also a number of interesting links between Samson and the movements of the Ark of God in the days of Samuel. Consider the following passages:

> "And there went from thence of the family of the Danites, out of Zorah and out of Eshtaol, six hundred men appointed with weapons of war. And they went up, and pitched in *Kirjath-jearim*, in Judah: wherefore they called that place *Mahaneh-dan* unto this day: behold, it is behind Kirjath-jearim."
>
> (Judges 18:11,12)

> "And the woman bare a son, and called his name Samson: and the child grew, and the LORD blessed him. And the Spirit of the LORD began to move him at times in the camp of Dan (RV, *Mahaneh-dan*) between Zorah and Eshtaol." (Judges 13:24,25)

---

5   If we are correct about the timing of Samson's birth then he would have been about eighteen years old at the time of this battle, therefore too young to serve in the army of Israel (Numbers 1:3,38, etc.).

"And the men of *Kirjath-jearim* came, and fetched up the ark of the LORD, and brought it into the house of Abinadab in the hill, and sanctified Eleazar his son to keep the ark of the LORD. And it came to pass, while the ark abode in *Kirjath-jearim*, that the time was long; for it was twenty years: and all the house of Israel lamented after the LORD."

(1 Samuel 7:1,2)

If Samson began to be moved by God's spirit in Mahaneh-dan (the camp of Dan), close to which was the Ark of God for twenty years, *was it this that encouraged him in his work of beginning to deliver God's people from the hand of the Philistines and in the twenty years of his judgeship?*

Compare the following map.

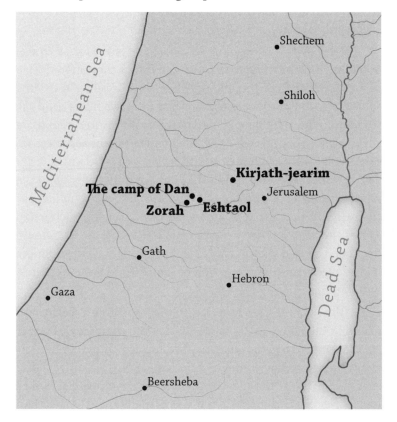

The return of the Ark

When the Ark was returned from the Philistines it was sent from Ekron to Beth-shemesh, which meant it would pass by, or through, Timnath (1 Samuel 5:10-6:12). "Beth-shemesh" means, 'house of the sun'. It stopped by the field of Joshua ('Yah saves') at the time of the wheat harvest (6:13,14). But God did not save, or deliver, Israel by this man from the house of the sun. Instead, the inhabitants of Beth-shemesh were punished for their mishandling of the Ark in some way that is not fully clear from the narrative, despite offering sacrifice to God, and rejoicing at its return (verse 13). Beth-shemesh was a city allotted to the Kohathites as recorded in Joshua 21:16. They of all people should have known how the Ark of God was to be handled for it was the Kohathites' responsibility to carry the items of the Holy Places (Numbers 4:15-20).

The Levites had set the Ark on a great stone for all to see, including the Philistine lords. Also the things they offered were unacceptable to God. They did not offer burnt sacrifices according to Leviticus 1. For the sacrifice they used the two heifers and the wood from the cart that was used to transport the Ark. Alongside this sacrifice they offered the golden emerods sent as a trespass offering by the uncircumcised Philistine lords (1 Samuel 6:14-18). It would seem that either they did not fully understand the true position of the Aaronic priesthood, and the true holiness of their God, or they chose to ignore the God-given instructions to Moses. Either way they were punished. The Ark of God should have been carried and covered from human sight. God's holiness had not been considered or respected since it had been taken into battle from its place in Shiloh.

The Ark was then taken from them to Kirjath-jearim and placed in the house of Abinadab ('father of generosity'). Eleazar ('God is helper') his son was sanctified to keep (guard) the Ark. It would appear to have remained there twenty years up until the events of 7:1,2. If our view of the chronology of this period of Israel's history is correct then it was actually there longer than that in total – even until David, the man after God's own heart, brought it to Zion (2 Chronicles 1:4).[6] The reason it was taken to Kirjath-jearim is not made clear in scripture. In fact from God's point of view this was the last place He would want the symbol of His dwelling presence to be. Kirjath-jearim, as we see from other references to it in scripture has associations with Baal worship. God's purpose in allowing the Ark to rest there for such a long time is something we are not told but as far as Samson is concerned it may, as we have already suggested, have provided added stimulus to his work as a saviour knowing how close the symbol of God's place of meeting with His people was in relation to himself.

There is, however, another possibility as to why the Ark ended up there. The places where Samson was moved by the Lord (Zorah and Eshtaol) were in fact in the portion of the land between the Ark's temporary home in Kirjath-jearim and the area of the land occupied by the Philistines who had captured it. Was Samson therefore being used by the Almighty to guard and protect the Ark until the Philistine domination of forty years came to an end as recorded in 1 Samuel 7?

What our suggested chronology means therefore is that about the same time the events in the early chapters of 1 Samuel took place, and in contrast to Joshua ('Yah saves') of Beth-shemesh ('house of the sun'), the Lord in His love for the people began to help them and so blessed Samson ('sunlight') from the tribe of Dan (judge), who was being moved by the Spirit of God *to deliver, or save*, Israel and bring judgement on the Philistines (Judges 13:5,24,25). Interestingly, one such judgement also took place at the time of the wheat harvest (15:1, RV).

So while the Ark of God was in Kirjath-jearim, and Samuel was growing up and being established as a prophet in Ramah and the area of Ephraim, God, through Samson, who shone forth as a saviour and a man of faith in a dark age, kept the Philistines at bay in the south-west of the land. God truly was Israel's helper. Later, the Lord was to use another man of faith, David, to bring to

---

6   Cf. also 1 Chronicles 15,16; 2 Samuel 6.

an end the Philistine stranglehold on Israel and to take the Ark of the God of Jacob to the habitation he had prepared for it in Zion.[7]

Like Samson and Samuel we live in a dark age when men and women in the main have turned their backs on their Creator. We, however, have been called out of darkness into the marvellous light of God's gospel of truth. And as the Master exhorted his disciples in his Sermon on the Mount, we too are to be lights shining forth for the glory of the God we serve (Matthew 5:14-16).

Psalm 78

Before we conclude this first chapter there is an interesting section in Psalm 78 that seems to recall the events of this time in Israel's history which is worth considering:

"So that he [God] forsook the tabernacle of Shiloh, the tent which he placed among men; and delivered his strength into captivity, and his glory [the Ark of God – 1 Samuel 4:21,22] into the enemy's hand. He gave his people over also unto the sword [1 Samuel 4:10]; and was wroth with his inheritance [Judges 13:1]. The fire consumed their young men; and their maidens were not given to marriage. Their priests [the sons of Eli, Hophni and Phinehas] fell by the sword; and their widows made no lamentation. Then the Lord awaked as one out of sleep, and like a mighty man that shouteth by reason of wine [Samson]. And he smote his enemies in the hinder parts:[8] he put them to a perpetual reproach."   (Psalm 78:60-66)

These verses from Psalm 78 would appear to support the interpretation that Samson and Samuel lived at the same time; and that Samson's work began after the capture and return of the Ark of God from the Philistines. Samson was God's "mighty man"; and the reference to wine is apt, because as we hope to show, drinking it was not a restriction placed upon him.

---

7   Cf. Psalm 132.

8   Compare Samson's attacks; also Genesis 49:16.

2 |

Samson from God's point of view

How God sees Samson – the divine perspective

BEFORE we look more closely at the record in Judges concerning the life of Samson, let us reflect on the divine perspective and consider him from God's point of vieww.

The Lord through Isaiah proclaims, "For my thoughts are not your thoughts, neither are your ways my ways, saith the LORD" (55:8).

Scripture is full of examples of the Almighty Lord God working out His purpose with men and women in ways we would never dream of. We might reflect on Abraham being called upon to sacrifice his only son Isaac when he had waited such a long time for the promised seed. Or think of all Joseph had to go through to become the saviour of his family. Consider too the life of Moses before he was ready to lead the children of Israel out of Egypt. Or David's experiences, graphically portrayed in his Psalms, before he became God's chosen king. What too of the experiences of the Apostle Paul or the Lord himself? The events that happened in their lives in order for God's purpose to move forward would, no doubt, not be the way we would have worked things out if we were providentially in control. But our ways are not God's ways, and His ways are not ours.

And so when we look at the record of the life of Samson let us not automatically look at the events in Judges 14-16 with the mind of the flesh but rather ask, why is God working this way in the life of the son He provided through a barren woman to be the saviour of His people? Let us view Samson from God's point of view, revisiting what scripture tells us about him.

Samson was a man of faith (Hebrews 11:32,39). Just consider the whole of this later section of Hebrews 11 and think of the record of Samson's life:

> "Who through faith subdued kingdoms, wrought righteousness, obtained promises, *stopped the mouths of lions*, quenched the violence of fire, escaped the edge of the sword, *out of weakness were made strong, waxed valiant in fight, turned to flight the armies of the aliens.* Women received their dead raised to life again: and *others were tortured, not accepting deliverance*; that they might obtain a better resurrection: and *others had trial of cruel mockings* and scourgings, yea, moreover *of bonds and imprisonment*: they were stoned, they were sawn asunder, *were tempted*, were slain with the sword: they wandered about in sheepskins and goatskins; being destitute, *afflicted, tormented*; (of whom the world was not worthy:) they wandered in deserts, *and in mountains*, and in dens and caves of the earth. And these all, having obtained a good report through faith, received not the promise: God having provided some better thing for us, that they without us should not be made perfect." (Hebrews 11:33-40)

Consider how many of these things recorded here in Hebrews 11 could be applied to the life of God's strong man of Israel. Surely we cannot doubt that Samson is one of the faithful of old who will not be made perfect till we too, in God's grace, will share in the fulfilment of the promises to the Fathers.

Why when we see such evidence in Hebrews does Samson get such a bad press?

Three key points to the life of Samson
There are three key points to the life of Samson that I believe resolve the negative statements that are made about him.

1. Samson is described as a man of faith – this is God's view
    of him.

    This does not mean that he had faith just before he
    died and so barely scraped into the list of the faithful in
    Hebrews 11. We need to look carefully at scripture and see
    what God has chosen to record about him and what He
    has left out. There is no record of the Lord condemning
    Samson for his actions (with one exception) – so neither
    should we.

    > "Be not deceived; God is not mocked: for whatsoever a
    > man soweth, that shall he also reap. For he that soweth
    > to his flesh shall of the flesh reap corruption; but he
    > that soweth to the Spirit shall of the Spirit reap life
    > everlasting." (Galatians 6:7,8)

    If Samson is listed among those who will reap eternal life
    through faith, and that is the divine view, are we right in
    condemning him as sowing to the flesh?

2. A clear understanding of what God meant for Samson
    to be a "Nazarite" is the key to answering many of the
    incidents recorded of him.

    We shall consider this in the next chapter of our study
    (page 25).

3. God's purpose was for him to *begin to deliver* his people
    Israel from their enemy the Philistines.

    He was given by God to be a *saviour* and God was to be with
    him and bless him as He was with all the judges (Judges
    2:18).[1]

We should be looking at the events of Samson's life with
these three key points in mind and not jump to conclusions
that he went completely off the rails in all he did, and so only
displayed the lusts of the flesh. As we have stated already, we
believe Samson was a man of faith who did fail, but whose life
has parallels to that of the Lord Jesus Christ in many ways.

---

1   Consider the list of times God was with Samson on page 20.

Questions relating to Samson

Let us consider a number of questions that we hope to answer as we study the scripture record in Judges. These are the main questions that caused me to revisit the Samson record.

1. Why does scripture place such emphasis on the revelation of Samson's birth by the angel and that the Lord blessed Samson as he grew if God knew he would be such a failure?

2. Was it necessary for Samson to be a tall, strong man with bulging muscles? The Philistines had giants living among them but as in the case of Goliath they were powerless before the likes of Caleb and David, men of faith, and Israel's God in whom they trusted. Note that the only references to Samson's strength are in Judges 16.

3. The three incidents involving women were only a small part of his life. Has God recorded them to warn us of the dangers of wrong sexual relationships *or* have they been recorded as part of God's purpose with Samson?

4. If Samson was so wayward in his actions why is there such an emphasis on the Spirit of the Lord coming upon him? Why also doesn't scripture record his repentance in order to be included in Hebrews 11?

5. How do we marry up God's command that Samson should be a "Nazarite" with His purpose for him to deliver Israel from the Philistines which would involve possible conflict, bloodshed and death, as was the case with the majority of the judges the Lord raised up to deliver His people Israel?

6. Why, if he was such a failure as a judge, does the scripture record tell us twice, that Samson judged Israel twenty years? What did he do during those years? Was he lusting after women and breaking the Law of Moses instead of serving God, or acting the part of a faithful saviour and judge?

7. Would God have allowed such an immoral, lustful and vow breaking man to judge His people for all that time if that was the kind of man he was?

8. Again, how could Samson pray to God as the Lord's servant and expect to be heard if he was such a wayward, godless character?

9. If Samson was the failure he is so often made out to be, why does scripture not condemn him for his actions instead of mentioning him amongst the faithful of Hebrews 11?

10. If he was a man of the flesh where is the evidence that justifies him being included in the hall of faith?

11. What then are the lessons for Israel and for us from Samson's one man confrontations with the enemy?

We must never forget God's commendation that he was *a man of faith*. Let's note also that in all the incidents recorded of Samson we see the hand of God at work strengthening him to punish the Philistines, but not condemning any of his actions until we come to the incident with Delilah.

The events recorded of the life of Samson

We now pause for a moment in our study and briefly list the events recorded of the life of Samson.

a. Announcement of his birth.

b. His mother to act like a "Nazarite", but not fully.

c. Birth and early life – Samson was to be a "Nazarite" – separated to God and blessed – The Spirit of God moves him.

d. He desires a woman of the Philistines – Why? – "Of the LORD".

e. Slays a lion – first show of God's strength in Samson – Why? – Is this a parable?

f. The feast, the riddle and betrayal.

g. Slays thirty men of Ashkelon – why Ashkelon?

h. Destroys the Philistine harvest by fire and slays more Philistines.

i. His rejection by his own countrymen – but slays a thousand Philistines with the jawbone of an ass.

j. Prays to God and is refreshed.

k. He judged Israel for twenty years.

l. Visit to Gaza – the harlot! – He removes the gates towards Hebron – Why? Is this another parable?

m. Samson loves Delilah and then reveals the secret of his strength – Another parable?

n. Samson's captivity and death, and killing of three thousand Philistines.

A small proportion of Samson's life

Why are only these incidents recorded of Samson? The events recorded in chapters 14-16 would only take up a small proportion of his twenty years of judging Israel, probably no more than a year or two of his life in total. What are we therefore to learn from them?

The usual, human, point of view is to condemn Samson for his failures to keep his vow because his life revolves around the lust for women. But is this true since there is no mention of him making a vow in the scripture record? Is this what God wants us to understand about His chosen saviour? As we have pointed out, there is no record of God condemning him, so are we right to do so? He did experience the frailty of his flesh, and he did sin, and the Lord did forsake him for a time, but then he died in faith.

Note also that these incidents fall into only six sections:

1. a and b – the promise of a saviour.

2. c – Samson's birth and early life – God is with His chosen saviour.

3. d-j – the occasion against the Philistines – the beginning of Israel's deliverance (these are all various incidents of one continuous episode).

4. k – Samson judges for twenty years.

5. l – Samson possesses the gates of Gaza.

6. m and n – Samson and Delilah – his capture and death.

Only sections 3, 5 and 6 give us any specific details of Samson's life and actions so we must be careful how we interpret them, remembering too that they amount to only a year or so of his life.

Key places in the life of Samson

Having thought about the incidents recorded, let us take a look at a map showing the places mentioned in the record of Samson.

We have already seen links between Samson and the movement of the Ark of God, but what of the other key places in the record of his judgeship? Are they significant? And if so why?

Note from the map there are only two of the five cities of the lords of the Philistines mentioned in the Samson record. We shall come back to why we believe this is so later in our studies.

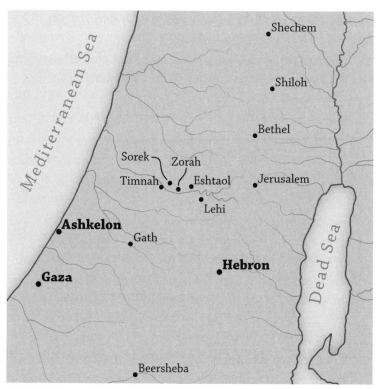

The other key place is Hebron which plays a prominent role in God's purpose and the promises He made to the fathers of Israel. Again we shall look at its significance in the Samson record later in our studies.

God at work in the life of Samson

Another thing we need to do before we proceed any further in our study is to note the number of times God plays a part in the record after Samson's birth. Compare the following details, some of which are direct interventions by the Almighty. But if Samson's strength did come from the Lord then the other incidents surely imply God's power being manifested through His chosen saviour.

"And the woman *bare a son*, and called his name Samson: and the child grew, and *the LORD blessed him*."   (Judges 13:24)

"*And the Spirit of the LORD began to move him at times* in the camp of Dan between Zorah and Eshtaol."   (verse 25)

"But his father and his mother knew not that *it was of the LORD, for he sought an occasion against the Philistines ...*"
(14:4, RV)

"*And the Spirit of the LORD came mightily upon him*, and he rent him as he would have rent a kid ..."   (verse 6).

"And *the Spirit of the LORD came upon him*, and he went down to Ashkelon, and slew thirty men of them, and took their spoil ..."   (verse 19).

"And *he smote them hip and thigh with a great slaughter*: and he went down and dwelt in the top of the rock Etam." (15:8 – surely this suggests God gave him the strength to do this)

"And when he came unto Lehi, the Philistines shouted against him: and *the Spirit of the LORD came mightily upon him*, and the cords that were upon his arms became as flax that was burnt with fire, and his bands loosed from off his hands." (verse 14)

"And he was sore athirst, and called on the LORD, and said, *Thou hast given this great deliverance into the hand of thy servant:*

and now shall I die for thirst, and fall into the hand of the uncircumcised?"   (verse 18)

"But *God clave an hollow place that was in the jaw, and there came water thereout*; and when he had drunk, his spirit came again, and he revived ..."   (verse 19)

"And Samson lay till midnight, and arose at midnight, and *took the doors of the gate of the city, and the two posts, and went away with them, bar and all, and put them upon his shoulders, and carried them up to the top of an hill that is before Hebron."* (16:3 – again how could he perform such a feat without God being with him and strengthening him?)

"... And she said unto him, The Philistines be upon thee, Samson. *And he brake the withs, as a thread of tow is broken when it toucheth the fire.* So his strength was not known."
                                                           (verse 9)

"Delilah therefore took new ropes, and bound him therewith, and said unto him, The Philistines be upon thee, Samson. And there were liers in wait abiding in the chamber. And *he brake them from off his arms like a thread."*   (verse 12)

"And she fastened it with the pin, and said unto him, The Philistines be upon thee, Samson. And he awaked out of his sleep, and *went away with the pin of the beam, and with the web."*   (verse 14)

"And she said, The Philistines be upon thee, Samson. And he awoke out of his sleep, and said, I will go out as at other times before, and shake myself. And he wist not that *the LORD was departed from him."*   (verse 20)

"And Samson said, Let me die with the Philistines. And *he bowed himself with all his might; and the house fell upon the lords, and upon all the people that were therein.* So the dead which he slew at his death were more than they which he slew in his life."   (verse 30)

In all the events recorded of the life of Samson we see the power of God at work. Samson's strength to achieve the things he did came from the Almighty. If Samson was a man of the flesh, would God have blessed him and strengthened him in the way He did?

Compare the words of Nicodemus about the Lord Jesus Christ "... we know that thou art a teacher come from God: for no man can do these miracles that thou doest, *except God be with him*" (John 3:2).

Once more we emphasise the clear message of scripture that God was with the saviours He raised up:

> "And when the LORD raised them up judges, *then the LORD was with the judge*, and delivered them out of the hand of their enemies all the days of the judge ..."   (Judges 2:18)

Surely it follows that *God was with Samson* and worked through the power of His Spirit upon him; and he, in turn, responded *in faith*, until, as we hope to show, he let his faith weaken at the hands of a self-seeking woman of the flesh – Delilah.

Bearing in mind all we have noted so far, and especially *the three key points* about Samson, let us now revisit the record in Judges 13-16.

However, before we do, compare the following chart concerning Samson and Jacob's prophecy.

Samson and Jacob's prophecy

- "Dan shall judge his people, as one of the tribes of Israel. Dan shall be a serpent by the way, an adder in the path, that biteth the horse heels, so that his rider shall fall backward." (Genesis 49:16,17)
- Compare this with the life of Samson.

  He judged Israel for twenty years.

  Samson made single-handed, serpent-like, attacks on the Philistines – but he would only start to deliver (save) Israel from them.
- This prophecy is followed by these words – a prayer?

- "I have waited for thy salvation, O LORD." (verse 18)

  Salvation: Strong's no. 3444 (feminine passive participle of 3467) – something saved, deliverance, hence aid, victory, prosperity.

  Samson was raised to begin to "deliver" his people from the Philistines.

  Deliver: Strong's no. 3467 – to be open, wide or free, that is to be safe, to free or succour.

- It is interesting that Jacob (under inspiration) inserts his *prayer* after his prophecy about Dan.

3 |

Separated to the Lord

Manoah and his wife

"And there was a certain man of Zorah, of the family of the Danites, whose name was Manoah; and his wife was barren, and bare not."
(Judges 13:2)

As we have seen already, Manoah was part of the remnant of the tribe of Dan left in the portion of land allotted to them in Joshua 19. His name means, 'rest', which is the opposite to many of the tribe who were restless and moved away north. Manoah's wife is not named but she is referred to as "wife" seven times in Judges 13, and to "woman" seven times. Perhaps this is significant as she was a faithful woman who was God-focused. She was barren[1] but was chosen by God to bear a son who was to begin to save Israel from the domination of the Philistines. The place where they lived was Zorah – the root word of which means 'wasp' or 'stinging'. Samson would go out from Zorah and inflict *stings* on the Philistines in order to bring *rest* to his people.

It would appear as we read though the record that Manoah and his wife were a godly couple. They perceived that the man who appeared to them was special. In fact he was an angel of God. They understood the conditions relating to the vow of a Nazarite – one who separated him or herself to the Lord; and also, as we

---

1   Note the double emphasis in verse 3.

read in Judges 14:3, about God forbidding marriage to the people of the land. They understood also about the sacrifices of the law, although they offered a burnt offering and not through a priest. When the angel appeared the second time, and then ascended to heaven in the flame of the sacrifice, Manoah was convinced it was an angel. But he also showed his weakness of faith compared to his wife:

> "And Manoah said unto his wife, We shall surely die, because we have seen God. But his wife said unto him, If the LORD were pleased to kill us, he would not have received a burnt offering and a meat offering at our hands, neither would he have shewed us all these things, nor would as at this time have told us such things as these." (13:22)

The visit of the Angel

The angelic visit to Manoah's wife, of the tribe of Dan (Judge) takes place at the beginning of the forty years of Philistine oppression (Judges 13:1). Israel did not cry to the Lord as on previous occasions; the cycle of Judges[2] is broken.

This time God acts – He shows grace to His people. Manoah's wife is barren but is promised a son. She is instructed to apply restrictions to her time of pregnancy that were included in the *voluntary* Nazarite vow detailed in Numbers 6. But this was not a voluntary decision on her part as the Nazarite Law specified. On this occasion it was a *command* from God Himself. Right away therefore we must beware of reading into the record what is not there. Remember it is the translators of the KJV and other versions who have chosen to transliterate the Hebrew word *nâziyr*[3] as "Nazarite" (or "Nazirite"). During her pregnancy the woman is told not to drink wine or strong drink or eat any unclean thing. She is to conceive and bare a son and no razor was to come upon his head and he was to be a *nâziyr* unto God from

---

2 The Judges Cycle = Sin – Suffering – Supplication – Salvation.
3 Strong's 5139 from 5144; separate, i.e., consecrated (as prince, a Nazirite); hence (figuratively from the latter) an unpruned vine (like an unshorn Nazirite).

the womb and he was to begin to deliver (save) Israel from the hand of the Philistines.

A Nazarite

First, we must take careful note of the content of the verses in Judges 13 that record the words of the angel, the divine message about Manoah's wife and her unborn son:

"And the angel of the LORD appeared unto the woman, and said unto her, Behold now, thou art barren, and bearest not: but thou shalt conceive, and bear a son. Now *therefore beware, I pray thee, and drink not wine nor strong drink, and eat not any unclean thing*: for, lo, thou shalt conceive, and bear a son; *and no razor shall come on his head*: for *the child shall be a Nazarite unto God from the womb: and he shall begin to deliver Israel out of the hand of the Philistines.*"   (13:3-5)

"But he said unto me, Behold, thou shalt conceive, and bear a son; and *now drink no wine nor strong drink, neither eat any unclean thing: for the child shall be a Nazarite to God from the womb to the day of his death.*"   (verse 7)

"And Manoah said, Now let thy words come to pass. *How shall we order the child, and how shall we do unto him?* And the angel of the LORD said unto Manoah, *Of all that I said unto the woman let her beware. She may not eat of any thing that cometh of the vine, neither let her drink wine or strong drink, nor eat any unclean thing: all that I commanded her let her observe.*"   (verses 12-14)

We now need to compare this information with what the Law of Moses said concerning the voluntary Nazarite vow.

We must remember initially that the Nazarite vow was intended for those who though unable, because of their birth, to be priests, were able to enact the role of a priest for a given period of time. They could, through fulfilling this vow be, for a set time, "*Holiness to the LORD*"; their uncut hair being a type of the mitre worn by the high priest. This, however, was not to be the role of Samson. He was to be a deliverer for his people not a priest.

As we see from comparing the two records, it does not specifically state that abstinence from drink and unclean things

---

The Nazarite Vow compared to Samson and his mother

Numbers 6:

- Voluntary.
- For a chosen period of time.
- No contact with vine, wine etc.
- There was to be no contact with death.
- The person's hair was to be uncut during length of vow.
- They were to be Holy to the Lord.
- There were processes to go through at the end of the period of the vow, or if the vow was broken.

Judges 13:

- *God decreed* that Samson and his mother should be "Nazarites" – it was *not voluntary on their part.*
- She must not drink wine or strong drink or eat any unclean thing.
- Samson's hair must not be cut and he is to be "one separated" unto God from the womb and shall begin to deliver Israel.
- We are not told specifically about abstinence of wine or of contact with death in relation to Samson.
- If he was to deliver Israel as the other "saviours" did, he would come into contact with death.
- Samson's uncut hair was meant to be an outward sign to himself and the people that God had 'separated' him to be their saviour. It was the sign that the Lord was to be with him.

---

applied to the son to be born. In fact there is no mention of a vow, or promise, on Samson's part as we have already stated. *The only condition* placed on Samson's separateness was the forbidding of the cutting of his hair. The other conditions associated with the voluntary Nazarite vow were placed on his mother (specified three times). For her the observing of these restrictions day by day would be a constant reminder of the special child she was carrying – the one God gave as her people's saviour.

But this was not the case with Samson. There were no further restrictions placed on him. If God was giving this son to be a deliverer, to begin to overcome Israel's enemies, then surely this would entail contact with slain men; with unclean bodies. The majority of the judges had to engage in war or conflict in order to save Israel from their oppressors. See the table below.

The Judges (saviours) and war

Judge	Reference	Oppressor	Outcome
Othniel	Judges 3	Chushan-rishathaim	Land had rest forty years
Ehud	Judges 3	Eglon king of Moab	Land had rest forty years
Shamgar	Judges 3; 5:6	Philistines	No mention
Deborah / Barak	Judges 4,5	Jabin king of Caanan	Land had rest forty years
Gideon	Judges 6-8	Midianites	Land had rest forty years
Tola	Judges 10	None mentioned	Judges twenty-three years
Jair	Judges 10	None mentioned	Judges twenty-two years

Judge	Reference	Oppressor	Outcome
Jephthah	Judges 11,12	Children of Ammon	Judges six years
Ibzan	Judges 12	None mentioned	Judges seven years
Elon	Judges 12	None mentioned	Judges ten years
Abdon	Judges 12	Amalekites?	Judges eight years
Samson	Judges 13-16	Philistines	Judges twenty years

Contact with dead persons would immediately affect, and compromise, the voluntary Nazarite vow made under the Law of Moses.[4] But this did not apply to Samson. Manoah's wife also adds information that is not given by the angel: that he was to be a *nâziyr* (separate to God) "to the day of his death" (13:7). There is no record of the angel saying this but she seems to understand that her child's work as Israel's saviour would end only at his death. Is this another indication of the spiritual mind of this woman and why God chose her (cf. verse 23)?

Many of the problems raised against Samson disappear if Yahweh intended him to be *a special Nazarite, or separated one.* If he was meant to be a true Nazarite, as in Numbers 6, then the whole of the period of his life we have recorded for us was a failure. But there is no record of him making such a vow, or of the Lord condemning him for not keeping it.

But if he was *a special Nazarite,* one separated, or consecrated, to God by the Lord Himself, then all the restrictions did not have to apply to him. The one about his hair was to be symbolic of his separation to the Lord and resulted in the strength of God being given him through the Spirit to overcome the enemy as his work moved forward. This itself is not stated by the angel, but is implied from Samson's own understanding of

4   Cf. Numbers 6:6-9.

this fact which he eventually reveals to Delilah and which will be considered in a later chapter (page 115). Only if he was *a special Nazarite* does it make any sense as to why so much emphasis is placed on God's Spirit coming upon him to overcome the Philistines and why the record emphasises the number of them he slew at his death (Judges 16:27,30).

We can find support for this interpretation of the inspired record from Rotherham's Translation:

> "And the messenger of Yahweh appeared unto the woman, – and said unto her – Lo! I pray thee thou art barren and hast borne no child, but thou shalt conceive, and shalt bear a son. Now therefore beware I pray thee and do not drink wine or strong drink, – nor eat anything unclean; for lo! thou art about to conceive and bear a son and no razor shall come on his head, for *one separate unto God* shall the boy be from his birth, – and he shall begin to save Israel out of the hand of the Philistines."[5]   (Judges 13:3-5, Rotherham)

If the other translations had not transliterated the word but translated it, as Rotherham does, then the misconception of Samson's life would, I believe, not be such a problem. Compare how we argue in a similar way concerning the problems that have arisen from commentators and other religious groups transliterating the Hebrew word *satan*, instead of translating it as 'adversary'.

Nazarites in the scripture record

The Nazarite vow was something to be freely taken for a short term, not something to be divinely demanded for a lifetime. There is no indication Samson took such a vow. The Rotherham translation confirms and supports the facts of Samson's life. If he was under *the Nazarite vow*, then as we have seen, his life would

---

5   Also compare The Bible in Basic English translation – "the child is to be separate to God". The NET Bible translation has "the child will be dedicated to God from birth". Note also Rotherham's translation of Samson's words to Delilah in Judges 16:17: "one separate unto God have I been."

be a dilemma and God's purpose with him a contradiction. But there is no mention of a vow. Commentators just assume there is because of the translators' use of the word Nazarite.

Compare the following chart.

The use of the Hebrew word *nâziyr*

- Strong's number H5139.
- Genesis 49:26 – "separate" – speaking of Joseph.
- Leviticus 25:5,11 – "thy vine undressed".
  The seventh year was a Sabbath to the Lord and therefore separated to Him.
- Numbers 6:2,13,18-21 – "Nazarite".
- Deuteronomy 33:16 – "of him that was separated" – speaking of Joseph.
- Judges 13:5,7 – "Nazarite" – Samson.
- Judges 16:17 – "Nazarite" – Samson.
- Lamentations 4:7 – "her Nazarites".
- Amos 2:11,12 – "Nazarites".
- In all these references 'separation' or being a 'separated one' is the key meaning of the word – it is not a title.
- It would seem there are no examples of a true "Nazarite" – one who separated him or herself to God for a period of time as described in Numbers 6 – in the whole of scripture. Compare also the panel relating to the Apostle Paul.

Nâziyr in scripture

Note from the chart that the same Hebrew word *nâziyr* is used of Joseph who was *separated* from his brethren (Genesis 49:26; Deuteronomy 33:16). God had also *separated* Joseph to be a saviour (Genesis 45:5-9). If the translators had not transliterated the Hebrew word in most of the passages it occurs, but had translated it as in the case of Joseph, then there would be less confusion in its application to Samson.

Note too that in the case of John the Baptist, when the divine message came to Zacharias about the birth of a son, only one of the Nazarite restrictions,[6] the one regarding wine, was to apply to him (Luke 1:15) even though, like Samson, he was given to a barren woman and *was separated* to God to begin a work of salvation to be completed by the Lord Jesus. And again this is specified by God through His angel: it was not voluntary on John's part.

Another difference between Samson and John is that concerning the Holy Spirit. In John's case Gabriel said, "He shall be filled with the Holy Spirit, even from his mother's womb" (Luke 1:15). But with regard to Samson it was as he grew up that the Spirit of the Lord began to move him. In John's case he was "the voice" through which the Spirit of God spoke. In the case of Samson, God's Spirit was seen through displays of physical strength.

With regard to Samuel, who again is considered to be a Nazarite, we have to read the record carefully to see what it says and doesn't say.

It was the faithful Hannah who chose to separate her son for the Lord's work; he did not make that choice himself. She too was a barren woman. If we are right in suggesting that Samson and Samuel were born about the same time, we could ask the question, did Hannah know of the circumstances of Samson's birth and the only restriction placed upon him by God regarding his separation for the work of saving his people? Was this why she said, "There shall no razor come upon his head" (1 Samuel 1:11)?

It is interesting to note that she uses the same Hebrew word for "razor" as used by the angel about Samson. These are the only occurrences of this term and is a different word from the

---

6   Interestingly John's work of baptism was handling the spiritually dead.

one used for "rasor" in Numbers 6:5 regarding the Nazarite vow. In addition to that, neither Hannah, nor the record in 1 Samuel, refer to her son as a Nazarite. It has only been suggested he was by commentators because of the reference to his hair. But there are no true scriptural grounds for assuming he was one.[7]

If we examine the scriptures carefully it would appear *there are in fact no true examples of a Nazarite* as described in Numbers 6 in the whole of God's word who are actually named. Nor in the examples that look on the surface as if they are Nazarites, are all the conditions of the Nazarite law met. Even the Lord Jesus himself, although he was *the separated one*, was not a true Nazarite in the sense of the law.

The two possible Old Testament exceptions to this are recorded in Amos 2:11,12 and Lamentations 4:7, and even in these examples individuals are not named, nor is it clear whether they were true voluntary Nazarites. In Amos the inspired prophet refers to the corruption of those in Israel who had been raised up to be Nazarites to God. Who they were, and how many of them there were, we are not told. The fact that it says God raised them up, as He had raised up those chosen to be judges, again makes it unclear as to the type of Nazarites they were. If they had chosen, or were ordained by God, to be separated to Him, they would have been a good influence and example to the people at large against a background of increasing evil. But even they had been led astray to unfaithfulness. So too in Judah, at the time the kingdom was nearing its end, there were those who chose to be Nazarites. But again they were corrupted. Once they were "white as snow", now they were "black as coal". Incidentally, Rotherham translates *nâziyr* in these two passages as "Nazarites", which suggests he thought they were true Nazarites in contrast to Samson who was a separated one by God.

The Hebrew word, as we have seen, is used of Joseph being separated by God. It is also used in Leviticus 25:5,11 of the vine

---

7   If Samuel was meant to be a life-long Nazarite then his 'vow' was broken when he slew Agag king of the Amalekites (1 Samuel 15:32,33).

which was separated out to be unpruned during the sabbatical year. This was part of the Lord's teaching in the Law of Moses that Israel was to be a holy, separate nation to Him.[8]

Key point

Once we have grasped this *key point* about Samson, many of the so-called difficulties of the record about him begin to disappear. Instead of seeing a man who plays fast and loose with God's law, we see, in fact, a man of faith separated to God for a specific purpose; one who, like all men except the Lord Jesus Christ, does sin and falls short of his calling, but nevertheless through faith completes the work God set before him.

As we asked in chapter two (page 16), was it necessary for Samson to be a giant of a man? The Philistines had giants living among them, but as in the case of Goliath they were powerless before the likes of Caleb and David, men of faith, and Israel's God in whom they trusted. Manly physique was not what set Samson apart from other men, or gave him the strength he needed to accomplish the tasks recorded of him. He was God-given, by the power of the Lord on a barren woman. He was *separated (or consecrated) to God for the purpose of being a saviour*. But also, for the spiritually minded Israelite of Samson's day, he was a living example of what the nation was to be – separate and holy to the Lord their God (Leviticus 19:2).

The principle of separation

Both Samson and the Lord Jesus had been separated for the Lord's work and were blessed by Him. So too were Israel as God's chosen people (Exodus 19:5,6; Deuteronomy 7:6-8). Under the law every man child born was to be holy to the Lord. But like Samson, the Lord Jesus Christ was especially born to be separate to his Father. The angel announced to Mary in Luke 1:35, "that

---

8   It is also worth looking up the associated Hebrew words for *nâziyr* in Strong to see the emphasis on separation and why the restriction concerning cutting the hair was symbolic. The notes on these Hebrew words are also worth reading in the *TWOT*.

Was the Apostle Paul a Nazarite?

The only two possible examples of one who took the "Nazarite" vow, or something similar, in the New Testament are recorded in the book of Acts and are in fact the only references to a vow in the KJV of the New Testament. Both relate to the Apostle Paul.

The first is in Acts 18:18 – "And Paul after this tarried there yet a good while, and then took his leave of the brethren, and sailed thence into Syria, and with him Priscilla and Aquila; having shorn his head in Cenchrea: for he had a vow." What this vow was is not clear; we can only surmise. In the case of a Nazarite vow the shaving of the head was a sign the vow was completed or broken because of defilement and in either case the shaving of the head was to be accompanied by sacrifices being made. This was not the case with Paul.

In Acts 21 we have the second incident. Having returned from his third missionary journey with the collection for the poor saints in Jerusalem, he is encouraged by the elders of the ecclesia there either to take a vow with four other men, or associate himself with them in their vow, in order to prove to the Jews that accusations made against him were false. "Do therefore this that we say to thee: We have four men which have a vow on them; *them take, and purify thyself with them, and be at charges with them, that they may shave their heads*: and all may know that those things, whereof they were informed concerning thee, are nothing; but that thou thyself also walkest orderly, and keepest the law ... and the next day *purifying himself with them* entered into the temple, to signify the accomplishment of the *days of purification, until that an offering should be offered for every one of them*. And *when the seven days were almost ended*, the Jews which were of Asia, when they saw him in the temple, stirred up all the people, and laid hands on him ..." (Acts 21:23-27). Whether or not this was the making of the Nazarite vow

> or one similar is not wholly clear. We are not given enough information to relate it to the details of the true Nazarite vow of Numbers 6. In Paul's case it was never completed for he was taken by the rioting crowd, who had been stirred up by the Jews of Asia, intending to kill him, but was rescued and arrested by the Roman soldiers stationed in Jerusalem (verses 27-34).

holy thing which shall be born of thee shall be called the Son of God". Twice in Acts 4 Peter, under inspiration, called the Lord "the holy child Jesus", and in chapter 2 he speaks of Jesus as God's Holy One who He would not allow to see corruption according to the prophecy in Psalm 16.

He was destined to be a high priest, "who is holy, harmless, undefiled, separate from sinners, and made higher than the heavens" (Hebrews 7:26).

That principle of separation applies in our lives too. Spiritually we are the Lord's chosen, holy and peculiar people (1 Peter 2:9). However, we have to be careful that we do not think we can do as we please. Liberty in Christ is not a licence to do what *we* think is right: "Use not liberty for an occasion to the flesh, but by love serve one another" (Galatians 5:13). God has called us out of the world of darkness and sin to be separate to Him, and has blessed us as He did Samson and the Lord Jesus. We are to 'be holy as God is holy' (1 Peter 1:15,16); the same principle that was taught to Manoah and his wife. The principle of deliverance by separation was taught in the life of Samson, and also by his mother, as they obeyed the restrictions placed upon them.

We therefore must seek to be faithful to our Heavenly Father at all times, always striving to do His will. Day by day, in faith, we must seek to remain separate and true to the Master we serve, not allowing the world to make us conform to its ways (Romans 12:1,2).

Samson's relationship with the Lord

After the first appearance of the angel to Manoah's wife and the instructions he gave to her, there seems, in subsequent verses, to be more in the record of Judges 13 that emphasises the special relationship Samson was to have with the Lord in his work as God's saviour.

Having been told by his wife of the visit of "a man of God", Manoah turns to the Lord and entreats Him (verse 8). The word "intreated" is the same Hebrew term used to describe Isaac praying to the Lord for his barren wife Rebecca. We can only imagine the surprise and joy Manoah must have felt on hearing this news. Note what Manoah asks of the Lord: to send the "man of God" again to "teach" them what they shall do with the child. Would he have asked this question if he understood that this God-given child was to be brought up as a "Nazarite", as depicted in Numbers 6?

In Judges 13, verses 6 and 7, when his wife recounts to Manoah the visit of the angel, she said she had failed to ask who had sent the "man", or his name, as she had been overawed by him and suspected he was in fact an angel. As we have already observed, in conveying the divine message to Manoah, she excludes the fact that the child is to begin to deliver Israel out of the hand of the Philistines but includes information not recorded as being spoken by the angel – that the child would be separated to God to the day of his death.

The word for "teach", used by Manoah in verse 8, has the initial idea of 'to flow as water (i.e., to rain); transitively, to lay or throw (especially an arrow, i.e., to shoot); figuratively, to point out (as if by aiming the finger), to'. This leads to the idea of 'to teach'. Manoah is therefore asking God what direction they should point their son in as he grows up. When the angel appears the second time and Manoah is able to communicate with him, he asks a similar question: "How shall we order the child, and how shall we do unto him?" (verse 12).

The Hebrew word for "order" is *mishpat* which has a root meaning 'to judge'. This is the word used more often for judgements or ordinances, especially those which God decrees for man to keep, as in the Law of Moses. The second half of the question in the KJV margin is, "what shall be his work?" The ESV translates the verse as, "what is to be the child's manner of life, and what is his mission?"

The answer, however, that Manoah receives from the angel does not include any further instructions, or information, regarding the son to be born. The only thing the angel emphasises relates to the restrictions on the woman during her pregnancy. Twice the man of God stresses to Manoah that his wife is to "beware" (verse 13) or "observe" (verse 14) all he has commanded. Those two words are the same in the Hebrew and mean 'to hedge about, to guard, protect, attend to.' The same word was used in verse 4 – again translated "beware". We see then the importance of observing God's command. The message of the angel emphasised how special and separate this child was to be. The fulfilling of God's commands by his parents would give Samson a wonderful example of faithful service to follow as he grew up to fulfil his God-given mission to begin to deliver Israel out of the hand of the Philistines.

But no extra information is given for the son to be born other than that given to Manoah's wife that he was to begin to deliver Israel out of the hand of the Philistines. Why we may ask? The answer it seems is at the end of the chapter and the beginning of chapter 14 which again supports the positive interpretation of Samson's life. It was to be the Lord God Himself who was to teach and "order" Samson as to what he should do. He was separated to God, he was the Lord's chosen saviour, it was God's spirit that would come upon him, and it was God's word he would fulfil. Manoah and his wife would care for his physical growth and set him an example of faithfulness to God's commands. We feel sure they would seek, as best they could, to fulfil the words of God through Moses recorded in Deuteronomy, "Hear, O Israel:

The LORD our God is one LORD: and thou shalt love the LORD
thy God with all thine heart, and with all thy soul, and with all
thy might. And these words, which I command thee this day,
shall be in thine heart: *and thou shalt teach them diligently unto
thy children*, and shalt talk of them when thou sittest in thine
house, and when thou walkest by the way, and when thou liest
down, and when thou risest up" (6:4-7). However, it was the Lord
who would instruct him spiritually regarding the work he was
destined to do. This was also the case with the one of which he
was a type (cf. Luke 2:39-52).

Teach them diligently to thy children

The examples of godly parents found throughout scripture
leave us with powerful lessons to learn from.[9] Our children, and
grandchildren, are faced with tremendous challenges from the
world in which we live. Godlessness is rife and they will need
the strongest foundation we can provide for them to be able to
make the right decisions when we are no longer there to hold
their hand.

Even the seedbed of the Bible, the creation record in the
early chapters of Genesis, is being questioned by those who
would have us accept a mixture of creation and evolution. These
are ideas that destroy the Bible's teaching of the origin of sin
and death "by one man" (Romans 5:12) and the doctrine of the
atonement through the saving work of the Lord Jesus Christ –
the one of whom Samson was a type.

The true foundation of our faith, wisdom and
understanding, can only be found in the scriptures. These words
of the wise man taken from the book of Proverbs provide, along
with many other scriptures, exhortation that is timeless for both
parents and children:

"Hear, ye children, the instruction of a father, and attend to
know understanding. For I give you good doctrine, forsake

9   Cf. Abraham as a prime example, Genesis 18:19.

ye not my law. For I was my father's son, tender and only beloved in the sight of my mother. He taught me also, and said unto me, Let thine heart retain my words: keep my commandments, and live. Get wisdom, get understanding: forget it not; neither decline from the words of my mouth. Forsake her not, and she shall preserve thee: love her, and she shall keep thee. Wisdom is the principal thing; therefore get wisdom: and with all thy getting get understanding. Exalt her, and she shall promote thee: she shall bring thee to honour, when thou dost embrace her. She shall give to thine head an ornament of grace: a crown of glory shall she deliver to thee. Hear, O my son, and receive my sayings; and the years of thy life shall be many. I have taught thee in the way of wisdom; I have led thee in right paths. When thou goest, thy steps shall not be straitened; and when thou runnest, thou shalt not stumble. Take fast hold of instruction; let her not go: keep her; for she is thy life."   (Proverbs 4:1-13)

But we must do more than just teach our children the things of God: we must be seen to be living them in our lives as examples to our children. The Lord we feel sure chose Manoah and his wife because He knew they would set the right example for Samson even though, as we have suggested, it would be God Himself who would teach him. He would have chosen them because of their faithfulness to Him and because of their spiritual understanding and application of the law.[10]

The angel's name

In the details that follow of the interaction between Manoah, his wife and the angel, we see how the angel turns their attention from himself to the Lord. It was God who had sent him and who should receive sacrifice and honour, not the angel himself. The record states that at this time Manoah still didn't understand

---

10 Note that in chapter 14 it is both parents who are closely involved in Samson's God-directed "occasion" against the Philistines. They are mentioned together seven times: Judges 14:2,3,4,5,6,9,16.

it was an angel who communicated with him. He spoke to him as if he were a man; he wanted to know his name. The answer given by the angel links with the main purpose of his message to this chosen couple that the son to be born to them was to be a separate one to God.

The angel said his name was "secret". The RV, and many other translations, have "wonderful". Strong's definition is "remarkable". It comes from a root word that appears in verse 19 – the word "wondrously" which means to 'be separate' i.e., 'distinguish'. This root word is used of the miracles or wonders God did in delivering the children of Israel from Egypt; and incidentally of the one who seeks to "separate" him, or herself, to make the vow of the Nazarite in Numbers 6:2. The Hebrew word for "secret" only occurs in one other place: Psalm 139:6. David here speaks of the omniscience of God who knows all his ways, his thoughts and words: "Such knowledge is too *wonderful* for me." There is, as David expresses in this Psalm, a great separateness, or distinction, between God and man. This is part of the wonder of who God is.

So it was in the revelation made to Manoah and his wife. The Lord was to show in a dramatic way this separateness, and the difference of this "man of God" who was in fact God's heavenly messenger sent by Him.[11] The miracle he performed was

11 Cf. Judges 13:19-23 with the visit of the angel of God to Gideon in Judges 6:19-23.

Separated to God "from the womb"
- Samson (Judges 13:5).
- Jeremiah (Jeremiah 1:5).
- John Baptist (Luke 1:15).
- Jesus (Isaiah 49:1; Luke 1:35).
- Paul (Galatians 1:15).
- Samuel given by Hannah to be separate to the Lord (1 Samuel 1:11,22,27,28)

to provide evidence that this was indeed a divine intervention in their lives. Also the acceptance of the sacrifice in such a miraculous way, and outside the normal stipulations for such sacrifices under the Law of Moses, was evidence, to the woman at least, that they would live to see the fulfilment of the promise regarding a son (verse 23).

In chapter 4 (page 45) we shall consider the relationship of the Lord with the son that was to be born.

The Lord and Samson

The birth of Samson

"And the woman bare a son, and called his name Samson: and the child grew, and the LORD blessed him." (Judges 13:24)

S AMSON was born of a woman, Manoah's wife, but we are not told her name. His name means 'sunlight' or 'shining'[1] and as we shall see Samson stood out as a shining light in a dark age.

The Lord blessed Samson

The record tells us Samson *"grew* and the LORD *blessed him"*.

No extra information is given about how Samson grew. We are not told anything about his physical form. We are certainly not told he grew into a muscular strong man for instance. Neither are we told about his character, whether good or bad – only that the Lord blessed him.

He is the only person in the whole of the book of Judges who it is said God blessed. The phrase, "the LORD blessed" is only used of four others:[2]

- Isaac – Genesis 26:12 (another child of promise).

---

1   Samson's name comes from the Hebrew word *shemesh* – meaning 'brilliant'. One use of this word is in Judges 5:31 at the end of Deborah's song which has an interesting link to Samson and his God-given strength.

2   The phrase is also used of God blessing the Sabbath day in Exodus 20:11.

- Potiphar's house (because of Joseph) – Genesis 39:5.
- Obed-edom – 2 Samuel 6:11; 1 Chronicles 13:14; 26:5.
- Job's latter end – Job 42:12.
- The phrase "God blessed" is also found in the following references: Genesis 1:22,28; 2:3; 9:1; 25:11; Deuteronomy 33:1; 1 Chronicles 26:5.

The Lord did of course bless others. For instance, similar words were used of Samuel, John the Baptist and Jesus.[3] Theirs were lives of faith; so why not Samson's? Why does scripture say the Lord blessed him and then record incidents of utter failure – if that is what they were?

It is interesting that in Numbers 6, after the details of the voluntary Nazarite vow, the Lord chooses to record through Moses how Aaron is to bless the children of Israel:

"And the LORD spake unto Moses, saying, Speak unto Aaron and unto his sons, saying, On this wise ye shall bless the children of Israel, saying unto them, The LORD bless thee, and keep thee: the LORD make his face shine upon thee, and be gracious unto thee: the LORD lift up his countenance upon thee, and give thee peace. And they shall put my name upon the children of Israel; and I will bless them."

(Numbers 6:22-27)

As Samson was to be *a special nâziyr* to God, and it specifically states the Lord blessed him, did this same blessing apply to him? If it did, then surely it shows how God was with Samson and blessed him as he did His work in faith. This emphasis seems to be overlooked by many commentators, and yet it has to be a key statement of the inspired record of God's dealings with the man He specifically raised up to be a saviour of His people. It is right at the heart of the life of this man, the anchor to which all else recorded of him is secured.

Despite his one failure to be true to his calling, at the end of his life God's countenance once more came upon him. God

3   1 Samuel 3:19; Luke 1:80; 2:40,52.

remembered him, and he was reconciled to the Almighty. In death he would have found peace of mind that the work God had raised him up to do was complete. Samson will also, with all the faithful, by God's grace, find an eternal blessing and peace in the day of resurrection when *the* Saviour returns.

Right from the beginning of creation the Lord has blessed those He created, especially those whose faith and trust are centred in Him, and who seek to walk in His ways. The Lord Jesus himself promised special blessings on those who followed him and displayed certain qualities in their lives. These of course are the 'Beatitudes' we find at the beginning of the Sermon on the Mount in Matthew 5:1-12 and also in Luke 6:20-22. To receive these blessings we must strive to display all the characteristics associated with them day by day as the Lord Jesus himself did in his life.

The Spirit of the Lord moved Samson

Not only does the record tell us the Lord "blessed" Samson but that he also began to "move him". Again this emphasises the special relationship the Lord had with him.

We made the point regarding the angel's answer to Manoah's question about how they should "order the child", that no extra instructions were given. Instead his wife was to beware, or guard, what the angel had given commandments to do. Now we see why. There was no need for further instructions concerning the son to be born. The Lord Himself was to "order" the child because He had separated him for His work.

And so it was that, "the Spirit of the LORD began to move him" (Judges 13:25). The Hebrew word "move" means 'to tap, beat, impel or agitate'. This word only occurs five times and in each reference it involves, or implies, the Spirit of God at work (Genesis 41:8; Judges 13:25; Psalm 77:4; Daniel 2:1,3). The first occurrence refers to Pharaoh being "troubled" by his God-given dreams that Joseph was able to interpret. The fourth and fifth occurrences are similar and refer to Nebuchadnezzar being "troubled" over his God-given dream of the image that Daniel reveals to him. The third occasion is in a Psalm of Asaph where the Psalmist is "troubled" as a result of God influencing his sleep. So in all these instances we see the hand of the Lord at work. Could the Lord have used the same method to "move" Samson? Did he have dreams or visions of the events that were to happen as God worked out His purpose with him? Compare also 2 Peter 1:21 where the Greek word "moved" means to 'bear, impel, or be driven' – a similar idea. This New Testament reference is in relation to those of the Old Testament in whom the Spirit of God worked.[4]

Whatever way God "moved" Samson, one thing is sure: His providential hand was at work. But God's deliverance of His people through Samson was to be different from that of other saviours He had raised up. Samson was not going to be the leader of an army, but was to do God's work of beginning to deliver His people single-handed. The people of God were so far from Him that there was no faith in them to follow a leader, or fight for the land He had promised to them.[5]

It took a special birth, and a special, separated man, for the Almighty to work out His pre-determined purpose of deliverance.

Samson would have been told by his parents of his special relationship to Yahweh and the work he was destined to do. So surely he would realise when the Lord "moved him" and the Spirit power of God was working through him that God was using him in His service. He would surely therefore believe and acknowledge, in faith, the blessings bestowed upon him; and would not be surprised later when the Spirit of God came mightily upon him as he played his role as the saviour of Israel from the Philistine lords and their people.

As we saw in the first chapter (page 8), the places between which Samson was moved by the Lord were the two cities of Zorah and Eshtaol, from which many in the tribe of

---

4   Cf. 2 Samuel 23:2; Nehemiah 9:30; Numbers 22:38; Jeremiah 20:9.
5   Cf. the events that develop in chapter 15.

Dan had left to migrate north where they took the city of Laish and renamed it Dan. Here we note again the contrast that the inspired word is surely teaching us. Samson's fellow tribesmen and women had migrated north through lack of faith in the Lord, who promised to be with them in striving to conquer the portion of the land allotted to them. But now God, through one chosen man – a man of faith – would display His power to begin to deliver His people from their enemy.

There should be no chapter break between Judges 13 and 14: this is one continuous record. God was ordering Samson's life and work. He blessed him and moved him by His Spirit. We have already seen (in chapter 2, page 20) how many times we are told the Lord was at work in Samson's life in relation to the Philistines.

> "*The* LORD *blessed him. And the Spirit of the* LORD *began to move him at times* in the camp of Dan between Zorah and Eshtaol. And Samson went down to Timnath (Timnah, RV), and saw a woman in Timnath of the daughters of the Philistines ... But his father and his mother knew not *that it was of the* LORD,[6] *that he sought an occasion against the Philistines*: for at that time the Philistines had dominion over Israel."
>
> (Judges 13:24-14:4)

"An occasion"

God (through Samson) "sought", or searched out, "an occasion" – an 'opportunity, or purpose' against the Philistines. Samson first went to Timnath and then saw the woman who was to play a vital part in God's "occasion". The inspired record is telling us that either God gave Samson instructions to go and take a Philistine wife – compare Hosea being told to marry a harlot, Gomer (Hosea 1:2) – or directed him by the Spirit; or that Samson chose this woman knowing of God's purpose with him. Either way this was in the purpose of God: it was sought for, it was "of the LORD",

---

6   Cf. Joshua 11:20.

even though under natural circumstances Israel were forbidden to make marriages with the Canaanite nations as recorded in Exodus 34:11-16 and Deuteronomy 7:1-6. It is interesting that in those passages the Philistines are not mentioned specifically by God. Could it be that in His foreknowledge He knew that Samson would be used to take a wife of the Philistines to accomplish His "occasion" against them in the days of the Judges? We cannot be dogmatic. Either we believe Samson disregarded God's laws given through Moses, which were clearly understood by his parents, or he acted fully aware that the Almighty was at work with him. The fact that the scripture record states in quick succession that the "LORD blessed him", and "The Spirit of the LORD began to move him"; and "it was of the LORD", surely implies Samson knew of God's purpose with him, and also that the outcome was that the Lord would use him to bring judgement on the enemy. Samson's actions were driven by faith in the purpose of the Lord with him, *not* by the lust of the flesh which God then used to achieve His purpose.

His parents, however, must have received a double blow to their own faith when Samson asked them to get this woman of Timnath for him. In their eyes he was not only going against God's commands given through Moses concerning making alliances with the people of the land, but he was actually asking to marry one of the very people from which he had been born to bring deliverance for his people. But they "knew not it was of the LORD".

Samson "went down", not in the sense of going away from God and seeking his own lustful pleasure, but in the sense of the topography of the land. This is illustrated in Judges 14:19 when it is said he "went up to his father's house"; also at the end of his life when his body was "brought up" to be buried in his father's grave (16:31). He "went down" into Philistine territory to do the Lord's work and to begin to deliver His people, not to satisfy the flesh.[7]

---

7   Compare these other Old Testament references where this same principle of God's purpose and providence is being worked out – Joshua 11:20; 1 Kings 12:15,24; 2 Chronicles 10:15; 25:20; 27:6.

The only other passage where we find the Hebrew word for "occasion" is Jeremiah 2:24. God through His prophet compares Judah to "a wild ass used to the wilderness, that snuffeth up the wind at her pleasure; in her *occasion* who can turn her away? All they that seek her will not weary themselves; in her month they shall find her". The context of this verse is the Lord's denunciation of His people for seeking and serving the gods of the nations around them. Israel had been planted as "a noble vine", verse 21; but now is compared to a wild ass in heat that sniffs out a mate. So God's people cannot be turned away from seeking an "occasion" to sin by lusting after, and worshipping, other gods. Interestingly in the context of the "occasion" God has with the Philistines, in Judges 14, we shall see that the vine and the ass figure in the types and lessons for Israel in the actions of Samson when the Spirit of the Lord comes upon him and he begins to deliver his people.

Note also the reason given for seeking this opportunity against the Philistines: "For at that time the Philistines had dominion over Israel" (verse 4). The word "dominion" means 'ruled or reigned'. This situation had arisen because Israel had done evil in the sight of the Lord. But Samson was given to begin to deliver them from this dominion. We said earlier that the events of chapters 14 and 15 are really one continual episode which begins with Samson going to Timnath and seeing a woman of the Philistines who he then seeks as a wife; and ends with him slaying a thousand of them with the jawbone of an ass. If we are right in interpreting the various incidents of this episode in this way, then it's interesting that the same Hebrew word for 'dominion' is found in what sparks off the final incident of this continuing episode in chapter 15. In Judges 15:11 we read:

> "Then three thousand men of Judah went to the top of the rock Etam, and said to Samson, Knowest thou not that the Philistines are *rulers* over us? What is this that thou hast done unto us? And he said unto them, As they did unto me, so have I done unto them."

Sadly the men of Judah had accepted this rulership of the Philistines and were even prepared to deliver their God-given saviour to the enemy rather than follow him in securing deliverance from those who had the dominion over them. We shall look at this again in chapter 5 (page 65). The two occurrences of this Hebrew word are, as it were, the bookends to the purpose God has against the Philistines, resulting in the loss of a thousand men and Samson judging for twenty years.

The woman of Timnath

The view of Samson that is commonly put forward is that he wanted this woman of Timnath because she pleased him, therefore leading to the conclusion his motivation was selfish lust. But the record does not say that he loved her, or lusted after her, even though she speaks of love in Judges 14:16. This contrasts with Samson's involvement with Delilah at the end of his life.

The margin rendering is, "Get her for me; for she is *right* in mine eyes". This is the same Hebrew word as "pleased ... well" in verse 7. Strong's Concordance gives the meaning as "a primitive root; to be straight or even; figuratively, to be (causatively, to make) right, pleasant, prosperous". This does not necessarily mean she was right, or pleasing, for a loving or lustful reason, but because it was the Lord's will for him.[8] It would provide an "occasion", an 'opportunity (for a quarrel)' (*TWOT*), against the Philistines. The events that grew out of the wedding, or betrothal, feast support this understanding of Samson's intentions. At that time, following the defeat by the Philistines at Eben-ezer (1 Samuel 4) the Israelites were demoralized; they didn't even pray to God for help. But God in His grace provided a way to *begin* to deliver them through *one man strengthened to work alone without the rest of the nation suffering.*

8   Note the end of verse 7 where it would appear that having "talked with the woman" she pleased Samson well. Whatever was said between them illustrated she was right for the purpose or "occasion" that was sought against the Philistines.

From the Philistines' point of view they would not suspect any ulterior motive in Samson's desire to take a wife from among them. God's people at that time had turned from God and were mixing with the inhabitants of the land, even to the point of worshipping their gods. To them, the desire of another Israelite to marry one of their own, would not therefore concern them initially – but all that was about to change. Despite Israel's failure to turn back to the Lord, He was beginning to initiate their deliverance.

Warnings and lessons

Although we do not believe Samson was seeking to fulfil the lust of the flesh in desiring a wife from the Philistine people; nor was he flagrantly disobeying the Lord's commands in associating with those who Israel were to destroy in the land of promise, we do acknowledge the warnings and lessons we can learn regarding union with unbelievers. Like Israel of old we need to beware of the dangers of uniting, in any way possible, with those who do not share our faith in Christ. Paul especially, in writing to Corinth, stresses this point and leaves us with a very important and powerful exhortation to heed:

> "Be ye not unequally yoked together with unbelievers: for what fellowship hath righteousness with unrighteousness? and what communion hath light with darkness? And what concord hath Christ with Belial? or what part hath he that believeth with an infidel? And what agreement hath the temple of God with idols? for ye are the temple of the living God; as God hath said, I will dwell in them, and walk in them; and I will be their God, and they shall be my people. Wherefore Come out from among them, and be ye separate, saith the Lord, and touch not the unclean thing; and I will receive you, and will be a Father unto you, and ye shall be my sons and daughters, saith the Lord Almighty. Having therefore these promises, dearly beloved, let us cleanse ourselves from all filthiness of the flesh and spirit, perfecting holiness in the fear of God."   (2 Corinthians 6:14-7:1)

Today, more than ever, this exhortation needs to be heeded by brothers and sisters of all ages and taught to our children as Samson's parents tried to do to him. His, though, was a special case – it was "of the LORD". His desire to take a wife of the Philistines was to set in motion God's purpose for beginning Israel's deliverance from their enemy.

Timnath

Timnath has already been mentioned in the scripture record. It occurs first in the book of Joshua in relation to the division of the land:

> "And the border ... *went down to Beth-shemesh, and passed on to Timnah* (Timnath): *and the border went out unto the side of Ekron* northward ..."   (Joshua 15:10)

This was Judah's border in the division of the land and should have been occupied by the children of Israel not the Philistines. Judah had been chosen by God to "go up; behold, I have delivered the land into his hand" (Judges 1:2). Like the rest of the tribes Judah had failed to conquer all the territory allotted to them.

But there is another possible link with Timnath in the record of the return of the captured Ark of God recorded in 1 Samuel 6:

> "And see, if it goeth up by the way of his own coast to Beth-shemesh ... And the kine *took the straight*[9] *way to the way of Beth-shemesh*, and went along the highway, lowing as they went, and turned not aside to the right hand or to the left; and the lords of the Philistines went after them unto the border of Beth-shemesh."   (verses 9,12).

The cart was loaded at Ekron (5:10-12), and sent on a straight course to Beth-shemesh, possibly via Timnah (Timnath). Beth-shemesh is just south of the camp of Dan; therefore as a young teenager Samson would surely know of this story of the Ark.

---

9   The Hebrew word for "straight" in 1 Samuel 6:12 is the same original word for "pleaseth me well" in Judges 14:3.

It is interesting to note that just as God providentially guided the oxen to bring back the Ark to Beth-shemesh past, or through, Timnah, so He was now guiding Samson along *the same road* to the *right* woman, that would bring about circumstances for His judgement on one more of the cities of the lords of the Philistines by God's strong man of Israel. These judgements that had begun when the Ark of God had been taken to three of those five cities during its captivity were to be completed by God through Samson. This is a key point which we shall deal with in a later chapter (page 95).

We can see from the map the proximity of the return of the Ark to the places where the Lord moved Samson.

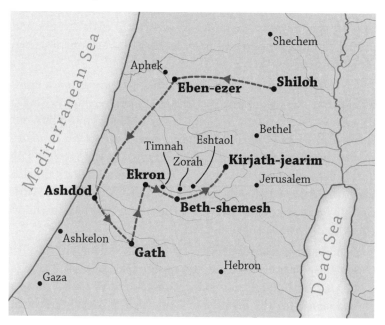

Samson and the lion

As Samson goes to commence his work as the God-provided saviour of Israel, by seeking a wife from among the Philistines, he is confronted by a lion. Why did the Lord in His providence allow a lion to attack Samson and then send His Spirit to enable him to slay it (Judges 14:5,6)? This would not make sense if Samson was supposed to be a true 'Nazarite' as outlined in Numbers 6. He would immediately be unclean, and his supposed vow of a Nazarite broken. His work for God would have to come to an end. His head would have to be shaven and sacrifices offered. Note that the word "body" – Hebrew *nephesh* – used in Numbers 6:6 can refer to humans or animals. But note also that the next time[10] Samson turns aside to see the lion he finds bees making honey in its carcass. This he takes[11] to eat and give to his parents. Why tell us this?

If we truly believe God was at work in the life of Samson, then we can see these things as more than events to provide a parable or riddle to outwit Israel's enemies and to bring about the "occasion" against them. These were providential events, and meant as a more important parable, first for Samson, and then for God's people to learn from.

Dan is described by Moses in his last words as "a lion's whelp that leapeth forth from Bashan" (Deuteronomy 33:22, RV). Now a descendant of Dan is attacked by a young lion but through the power of God upon him overcomes it. In this case the young lion represents Israel's enemy, the Philistines. The lion is used elsewhere in this way (e.g., Jeremiah 2:15; cf. also Proverbs 28:15). Samson himself represents Israel who, with God-given strength, can overcome the enemy that has dominion over them. Compare Joshua 23:

> "And ye have seen all that the LORD your God hath done unto all these nations because of you; for the LORD your God is he that hath fought for you ... One man of you shall chase a thousand: for the LORD your God, he it is that fighteth for you, as he hath promised you."   (verses 3,10)

Samson slew the lion in the vineyards of Timnath. "Timnath" means 'a portion assigned', and so is representative of the whole land. The vine was a symbol of Israel, who God planted

---

10 Obviously some weeks or months later.
11 Again this would have rendered a true Nazarite unclean.

in the land (Psalm 80:8,9; Jeremiah 2:21). This too fits nicely into this greater parable. The outcome for Samson of his encounter with the lion is that sometime later when he visits the site of the lion's carcase he finds honey that he is able to take from it to eat. The significance of the parable for the people of Israel, who were represented by Samson,[12] would be a time of sweetness and fellowship with God, just like honey. This would be the blessing, if they fought against their enemies, knowing that the Lord had promised to be with them. This would fulfil the promise of the Lord in Exodus 3:8,17 that the land He would give them was "a land flowing with milk and honey".[13]

Another point worth noting is the use of the original word for "carcase" elsewhere in the Old Testament. This in fact is the first occurrence of the Hebrew word, which Strong defines as "fall, that is decadence, concretely a ruin specifically a carcase". The word is used once in Proverbs to describe the fall of the wicked which the righteous shall see (Proverbs 29:16). All six other occurrences are found in the prophecy of Ezekiel and describe the "fall" or "ruin" of the Gentile nations as a result of God's judgements upon them. This surely adds weight to our proposition that the lion represents the nations at enmity with God's chosen people.[14]

But there is a further interesting link with the honey and the lion being part of this parable for Israel to learn from. In Judges 14:9 we are told that Samson "*took* (the honey) thereof" and gave to his parents, "but he told not them that he had *taken* the honey out of the carcase of the lion". According to Strong

---

12 A further connection with Israel is the fact that the Hebrew word for "swarm", relating to the swarm of bees, is the word used over a hundred and twenty times to describe the "congregation" or "company" of Israel (cf. Exodus 12:3,6,19, etc.). This occurrence in Judges 14:8 is the only time it is not used of people.

13 This description of the land is used twenty times in the Old Testament and in the last two, in the prophecy of Ezekiel, God adds the words "the glory of all lands" (Ezekiel 20:6,15).

14 This original term applies to the first word for "carcase" in Judges 14:8. However, the second occurrence and the one in verse 9 is a different Hebrew word which means 'body either alive or dead'.

these two words are a translation of the Hebrew word *raw-daw'*, meaning "to tread down, i.e., subjugate; specifically, to crumble off". *BDB* says the word means "to rule, have dominion, dominate, tread down, also to scrape out". This is the word used in Genesis 1:26,28 of God's creation of man and woman having "dominion" over the rest of His creation. It is used also of the Messiah who will "have dominion also from sea to sea and from the river unto the ends of the earth" (Psalm 72:8). Was the scraping out of the honey from the carcase of the lion meant to signify again the fact that if the people acted in faith and fought against their enemy the Philistines, they too would have dominion over them as God intended they should?

Samson's confrontation with the lion is the first of the occasions when the Spirit of the Lord comes upon him. It tells us he rent the lion as he would have a kid with nothing in his hands, emphasising that it was God's power that wrought the victory. But note that it says God's Spirit "came mightily" upon him. The original Hebrew word is used three times of Samson. The other two occurrences are in chapter 14:19 where it is translated "came", and chapter 15:14 where it's rendered again as "came mightily". According to Strong the word means "to push forward in various senses". *TWOT* defines it as "prosper, succeed, be profitable". It then has this comment: "The root word means to accomplish satisfactorily what is intended. Real prosperity results from the work of God in the life of one who seeks God with all his heart."[15]

This word is used of Hezekiah in 2 Chronicles 31:21; of Joshua in Joshua 1:8; the Psalmist (Christ) in Psalm 1:3; and of God's word in Isaiah 55:11. It is also used of God's work through *the* Saviour in Isaiah 53:10. Its use in connection with the Spirit of God coming upon Samson surely points to a man of God being used by the Almighty to accomplish satisfactorily His purpose of deliverance through His chosen saviour; a man who, so far, sought the Lord with all his heart.

---

15 *TWOT* number 1917.

Samson's silence

Note also there are two other important points in the narrative
that follow on from the slaying of the lion. First, Samson does not
tell his father and mother about what he had done, or where the
honey he gives them had come from. It is usually thought that he
kept quiet about it because he had already broken the Nazarite
vow placed upon him. However, we have already seen from chapter
13 that there was no vow made by him. If, however, we look at
the next point the narrative tells us, we can see that Samson's
silence was probably for a more important reason. Judges 14:10
tells us his father went down to the woman. He went to make the
wedding arrangements, presumably according to the customs of
that time. According to the same customs Samson makes a feast.

In verse 11 we read, "And it came to pass, when they saw
him, that they brought thirty companions to be with him". The
word "they" must surely refer to the Philistines, perhaps even
some of their leaders or lords. What did they see about this man
from Israel apart from his long uncut hair that caused them to
bring these thirty men to accompany him? We are not told. But
who were they? In verse 16 we have the answer when his "wife"
says to him "... thou hast put forth a riddle unto the children of
my people ..." These "companions" were Philistines as verse 18
also makes clear. The Hebrew word only occurs seven times and
four of them relate to Samson's companions. It comes from a
root word that Strong says is "a primitive root; to tend a flock;
i.e., pasture it; intransitively, to graze (literally or figuratively);
generally to rule; by extension, to associate with (as a friend)".
Were these men given to Samson to watch over him as a shepherd
does his sheep? Were they now suspicious of this man from
Israel? Were they there to guard him, not from danger to himself,
but to guard their people from him? We cannot be certain: but
the one thing we can be sure of is that God was the true overseer
of the situation, and these thirty men were to play an important
part in the purpose Yahweh had to begin to deliver His people
from the Philistines through Samson.

During the feast Samson puts forth a riddle and a wager to these thirty men. The answer to it lay in his slaying of the lion and the honey that came from its carcase. If he had told his mother and father about these things then it is possible they may have let slip this information and so the desired effect of the riddle would be lost. Remember all of this is "of the LORD" who is seeking, through Samson, an occasion against the Philistines, something Samson's parents knew nothing about. In God's purpose with him it was to be a Philistine woman who would play the key role in revealing the meaning of the riddle, and so bring judgement on her people when again the Spirit of the Lord would come upon Samson.

If these thirty men could tell Samson the answer to the riddle within the seven days of the feast he would give to them thirty sheets and thirty changes of garments, one each. But if they could not provide the solution in the set time they were to pay him thirty of each instead. The Hebrew word for "sheets" according to Strong is, "to envelope; a wrapper, that is a shirt". In Proverbs 31:24 and Isaiah 3:23, the only other occurrences of the word, it is translated "fine linen". The word for "garments" has an interesting meaning considering the outcome of events. The meaning given by Strong and *BDB* is "a covering (garment) or treachery, pillage or deceit". How appropriate, considering what developed as a result of the bribery of Samson's "wife". But when we think of the number thirty and treachery surely our minds go forward to Judas' betrayal of the Lord Jesus for thirty pieces of silver. And so the riddle was put to them: "Out of the eater came forth meat, and out of the strong came forth sweetness" (Judges 14:14).

Samson, his 'wife' and the riddle

Having set the riddle[16] for his thirty Philistine companions, based on his slaying of the lion and the finding of the honey, Samson eventually submits to his wife's pleadings to explain it

---

16 Strong: "a puzzle, hence a trick, conundrum, sententious maxim."

to her. The Philistines, who were running out of time[17] to solve it, and were upset that they would be impoverished as a result of being unable to give to Samson the answer to the riddle, had threatened to burn her if she failed to entice him into revealing its secret (verse 15). The record tells us she "wept" and "lay sore (to compress, i.e., [figuratively] oppress, distress) upon him" until he told her, and then she betrayed him (verses 17,18). The result though was in the providential hand of God. Because these thirty men had, as Samson put it, "plowed with my heifer" (verse 18), they had in effect brought about the opportunity God required for the saviour He had raised up. The Hebrew word for "plowed" is an interesting word. The *TWOT* says, "the basic meaning is cutting into some material e.g., engraving metal or ploughing soil". It's used in scripture in other places, as it is here, in a figurative way to describe 'devising', especially secretly and usually in connection with evil. According to Strong and *BDB* it is also translated in relation to non-communication, expressed by either not speaking or not hearing. We shall come across the word again in this second sense in chapter 16 in relation to Samson going to Gaza.

And so the next stage of Samson's work and God's "occasion" against the Philistines takes place, as once again the Spirit of the Lord came upon him and he went down to Ashkelon and there slew thirty men in order to pay the wager of the riddle (verse 19). This is the second time we are specifically told "the Spirit of the LORD came (RV, mightily) upon him". Clearly God was at work with the saviour He had given to begin Israel's deliverance.

Why Ashkelon?

Why though did he go to Ashkelon? This city was some thirty miles away from Timnath. Surely there was somewhere nearer?

---

17 Note that the RV margin of Judges 14:15 says that rather than being the seventh day it was the fourth day. This seems to make more sense of the timing of their threat to Samson's "wife". Also the KJV marginal note for verse 17 says, "or the rest of the seven days".

Ashkelon was one of the two remaining cities of the lords of the Philistines not to be judged by God after they had taken the Ark of the Lord at the battle of Eben-ezer (1 Samuel 4).[18] "Ashkelon" means 'a weighing-place (i.e., mart)'. It comes from a root word meaning 'to suspend or poise (especially in trade)'. It's interesting that this root word is the one used in Zechariah 11:12 in the prophecy relating to Judas' betrayal of Jesus for thirty pieces of silver.

So Samson slays thirty men of Ashkelon and takes their "spoil", pays his wager and then returns home to Zorah (verse 19). He had, through God's power coming upon him, inflicted the first of his stings against the Philistines. But there is possibly another reason why Samson was guided by the Spirit to Ashkelon that comes to light if we look at the meaning of the Hebrew word for "spoil" and its associated root words. The Hebrew word only occurs in one other place (2 Samuel 2) where we read of David's nephew Asahel pursuing Abner the son of Ner.

"And Abner said to him, Turn thee aside to thy right hand or to thy left, and lay thee hold on one of the young men, and take thee his *armour*. But Asahel would not turn aside from following of him."   (verse 21)

This word comes from the Hebrew term meaning 'strength', which in turn comes from the primitive root which Strong says means "to pull off; hence (intensively) to strip, (reflex.) to depart; by implication, to deliver, equip (for fight); present, strengthen". *TWOT* says it means "what is stripped off a person, as plunder, in war". So too the *BDB* definition: "what is stripped off (a person in war), armour, spoils, belt." These meanings suggest that perhaps these men Samson slew were in fact Philistine soldiers. If this were so then an initial blow was made against the Philistine army, and God's strong man overcame the strong men of Israel's oppressors. The "spoil" therefore could well have been part of their armour, or clothing as soldiers.

---

18 See later in chapter 7 (page 95) the reason why Samson goes to Gaza.

Samson's anger

The outcome of giving the changes of garments to those who expounded the riddle was that "his anger was kindled" (Judges 14:19). There are a number of possible reasons for this. Was he angry with the men who were responsible for threatening his "wife" that led to him slaying thirty men? Was he angry because his "wife" had revealed the answer to them? The Hebrew word for "wife" is translated wife or woman and so we cannot be certain that Samson had actually consummated his marriage to the woman of Timnath (note the early verses of chapter 15). Whether he had or not, as we have already seen, the whole situation was in the providential hands of God.

Or was Samson's anger, righteous anger, when he contemplated the fact that the enemy was still in the land of promise which his own people had failed to conquer? The very Philistine city he had been directed to by the Spirit, to slay thirty of their men to provide the garments to those who had threatened his "wife", was in fact the second of the cities of the Philistines that had once been taken by the tribe of Judah. But in the time of Samson it was back in enemy hands through the weak faith of God's chosen people.

Whatever the reason for Samson's anger, this was all part of God moving him to bring about a situation that was to lead to further judgements on the Philistines. Those judgements were soon to follow because Samson's "wife" was given to his companion – best man (verse 20) – as we shall see by considering Judges 15.

Samson went up to his father's house

We have seen that it was the providential hand of the Lord that was behind the events of Samson's life so far. Samson had lived with his parents in Zorah and had been blessed by the Almighty. He had been moved by the Spirit of the Lord between there and Eshtaol. He had gone down to Timnath from his father's house and desired a wife of the Philistines according to God's purpose with him to begin to deliver His people from the dominion of their enemies. But having brought judgement on the city of Ashkelon, and having paid the wager concerning the riddle, he doesn't at this time return to the woman he desired to marry, but to his Father's house. He went down to Timnath but now he goes up, back to his home in Zorah. He returned to where the Spirit of God had begun to move him. As a man of faith he could now reflect on what he had done so far in the Lord's service and how God's Spirit power had worked through him. He may have spent time in prayer seeking guidance as to what to do next.

What happened next we shall consider in chapter 5 (page 65).

The Father's "house"

There may be times and circumstances in our lives when we are driven to anger or wrath. These are characteristics we are called upon to put off having been raised with Christ through the waters of baptism (Colossians 3:1,8).[19] The solution is to put on the characteristics of our Heavenly Father and His Son; to set our minds on heavenly things not on earthly (verse 2). This of course does not come naturally. We need therefore to go constantly to our Father's "house", into the very presence of heaven itself, through our mediator at His right hand and spend time there in contemplative prayer. Only through prayer, and guidance from the inspired word of life, can we overcome the fleshly characteristics that so easily beset us. We must look to our Lord's example, and remember that the Almighty God we serve is the One who is "... gracious, and full of compassion; slow to anger and of great mercy" (Psalm 145:8).

---

19 We may at times think our anger is justified, and in fact is righteous anger as the Lord Jesus himself displayed, when he drove out the money-changers and said to them, "Make not my Father's house a house of merchandise". But is it? Cf. *The Letter to the Ephesians*, Brother John Carter, pages 125-128.

The destroyer of our country

Samson's retribution

T HE events of chapters 14 and 15 are one continuous episode. The "occasion" the Lord had against the Philistines was not fulfilled by the events recorded in chapter 14.

We have to keep in mind God's purpose with Samson as we consider the events of chapter 15 and not look at what is recorded of him as if he is running wild, doing his own thing, and acting in a lustful and vengeful way without regard for Yahweh his God. They are all part of God's "occasion" against the enemy, and Samson is God's appointed saviour.

After spending some time back in his father's house, Samson returned to visit his "wife" in Timnath. We are not told how long a period of time elapsed between the events in chapter 14 until he returned there. Did he go to consummate his marriage to the woman of Timnath which was "of the LORD" (Judges 15:1)? All we are told is of his intention to go into his wife in her chamber. Whatever the reason, he was not allowed to see her by her father. His wife had been given to another on the assumption that Samson hated her (14:16; 15:2).

But as the record goes on to reveal, the giving of Samson's "wife" to another man enables God's purpose to begin to deliver His people from the Philistines to take another step forward. Samson sets about taking retribution rather than satisfying his

so-called lust with another woman of the Philistines, if that's all
his life was about (verses 2,3).[1]

Compare *YLT* of verse 3: "And Samson saith of them, 'I
am more innocent this time than the Philistines, though I am
doing with them evil'." The Hebrew word for "more innocent", or
"more blameless" (KJV), is the same word used in the revelation
of God's name to Moses in Exodus 34:

> "Keeping mercy for thousands, forgiving iniquity and
> transgression and sin, and that will *by no means clear* the
> guilty; visiting the iniquity of the fathers upon the children,
> and upon the children's children, unto the third and to the
> fourth generation."   (verse 7)

It is also used in Proverbs 6:

> "So he that goeth in to his neighbour's wife; whosoever
> toucheth her shall not be *innocent*."   (verse 29)

From a natural point of view Samson was the innocent
party regarding the giving of his "wife" to another man. The
father who had given her to another, and the man who had taken
her, were not innocent. But God was at work behind the scenes:
and through these events relating to Samson seeking a wife of
the Philistines the Lord was able to bring further judgement
on Israel's oppressor. In fact it may be that it was the Lord that
Samson addressed when he spoke the words of verse 3. The
record is not specific as to whom he was addressing.

Samson brings a kid

We are told two facts in Judges 15:1. Firstly it was the time of the
wheat harvest[2] – the time of the Feast of Weeks; secondly Samson
visited his "wife" with a kid. These facts must be seen as part of
the "occasion" against the Philistines. Was Samson being moved

---

1   If Samson was the strong man who lusted after Philistine women as portrayed in
    other commentaries, why didn't he use his strength to overcome his father-in-law
    and take back what was rightly his?

2   This piece of information sets the scene for why Samson's actions recorded in the
    following verses were so devastating.

to act in a way that would result in God's purpose being fulfilled? Many commentators suggest the kid was a conciliatory gift for his "wife", or for a meal they would share at the consummation of the marriage. On the occasions this Hebrew word for kid is used, it usually has to do with food. The only exceptions are Judges 14:6 in relation to the young lion Samson slew (which we have suggested is a symbol of the Philistines), and Isaiah 11:6, a picture of the peace of the kingdom which can be read as literal, or symbolic of the nations. As the events unfold this kid was not used for food: instead what happens in the record is a fulfilment of what we believe the incident of Samson and the lion represented. Through the Spirit of God coming upon him Samson had rent the lion like a kid. Soon he was to do the same to over a thousand of the Philistines after he first destroys their harvest and brings upon them a great slaughter.

Consider two more interesting facts. Under the Law of Moses a kid of the goats (both male and female) played important roles in the nation's sacrifices offered to the Lord. The kid of the goats was used as a sin offering as part of the sacrifices offered during the Feast of Weeks (Leviticus 23:19). The kid of the goats was also the offering that the ruler who had sinned was to make as a sin offering, as specified in Leviticus 4:22-26.

Is there a link with Samson's words of being more innocent than the Philistines in Judges 15:3? He had been raised up to do God's work as His chosen judge, or ruler, and would not therefore be sinning and so have to offer the kid in sacrifice. We cannot be sure what his purpose with the animal was, but in what is about to unfold he himself declares he is innocent, even though he will do them displeasure.

Samson's words about being more blameless may also have reference to one of the judgements God gave to the children of Israel at Mount Sinai. In Exodus 22 God declared:

> "If fire break out, and catch in thorns, so that the stacks of corn, or the standing corn, or the field, be consumed therewith; he that kindled the fire shall surely make restitution." (verse 6)

In the case of Samson, he was not going to pay restitution as he was not acting against his own people. He would therefore be blameless in his actions against Israel's enemy as he did them displeasure. He was avenging the oppression of his people by the Philistines. This was to be part of God's purpose against them.

And so it was that as a result of these events Samson wreaked havoc with the Philistine harvests using firebrands, or torches, tied to the tails of foxes. He not only destroyed "the standing corn" he also set fire to "the shocks", the stacks of sheaves, with the "vineyards and olives". This would be a great blow to the Philistine economy. We are not told how much of the Philistine territory was devastated by this fire but it must have been extensive considering the number of foxes used. All the things that were destroyed were essential parts of their livelihood; they were things that provided food and drink and fuel for cooking and light. God's strong man of Israel, whose name signified 'light', put the enemy of Israel into darkness and despair. No wonder the Philistines later describe Samson as "the destroyer of our country" (Judges 16:24). The Hebrew word for "destroyer" means 'to parch (through drought), i.e., (by analogy), to desolate, destroy, kill' – a very appropriate word for what the fires started by Samson, and the foxes, would do to the ground after they had burnt everything in their path.

Samson's use of firebrands and foxes

Why did Samson choose this way to bring judgement on Israel's enemy? It would have been no mean feat to capture these three hundred creatures in the first place, let alone do what he did with them to cause havoc among the Philistines and stir up hatred against him. This was no foolhardy act, but was done in faith as part of his work as Yahweh's deliverer.

Samson used three hundred foxes. Was this meant to be significant? Compare Gideon using only three hundred men to overcome the Midianites (Judges 7:16). This had been a divine directive to Gideon as it was to be through the Lord's power and intercession that victory over the Midianites was to be accomplished (verse 22). We have already seen the Lord also at work through Samson. Was God again providing for Israel another reminder of what could be achieved if they only put their trust in Him and went out against their enemies as He had commanded them to do through Joshua?

The Hebrew word for "foxes", "a jackal (as a burrower)" according to Strong is "from an unused root meaning, to hollow out; the palm; by extension, a handful". This root word is only used three times.

In one occurrence it is used of the Lord in Isaiah 40: "Who hath measured the waters *in the hollow of his hand ...*" (verse 12).

The occurrences of "fox" in scripture portray an animal that is related to destruction and desolation: the very thing Samson was accused of doing to the country of the Philistines.

But what of his use of firebrands; were Israel, and ourselves, meant to see a deeper significance in their use? The word for "firebrands"[3] occurs fourteen times in the Old Testament record, three of which are here in Judges 15. Fire in scripture is often used for judgement as well as the presence of God. An example of this can be found in the early chapters of Amos where God, through His prophet, predicts judgement on His people and their surrounding neighbours by fire (Amos 1:4,7,10,12,14; 2:5; 5:6).

Of the remaining eleven occurrences of the Hebrew word for "firebrands" two are found in the poetic language of the book of Job. The remaining nine occurrences have a reference to God, or His work.

The first occurrence is in Genesis 15:17 – "a burning lamp" – this was a symbol of the presence of God as He makes His covenant with Abraham concerning the Promised Land.

The second occurrence is in Exodus 20:18 – "lightnings" – this was part of the description of the manifestation of God

---

3 Strong's meaning – "from an unused root probably meaning to shine; a flambeau, lamp or flame – a torch".

at Mount Sinai when He makes a covenant with Israel and gives them the Ten Commandments.

In Judges 7:16,20 it describes the "lamps" or torches used by Gideon and his three hundred men to bring judgement on the Midianites. Did this incident inspire Samson to use three hundred foxes to bring judgement on the Philistines?

In Isaiah 62:1 God foretells that in relation to His purpose with Zion and Jerusalem 'salvation will go forth as a lamp'.

In Ezekiel 1:13 in the vision of the glory of God the appearance of the living creatures was like "lamps".

In Daniel 10:6 it is used as part of the description of the symbolic man Daniel sees in a vision. This man has eyes "as lamps of fire".

In Nahum 2:4 it is translated "torches" – and is used to describe part of the time of judgement God brings on His people.

The last occurrence of the word is an echo of the judgement God brought on the Philistines through Samson. Zechariah 12 describes events in the last days of God's purpose with Jerusalem:

> "In that day will I make the governors of Judah like an hearth of fire among the wood, and *like a torch of fire in a sheaf*; and they shall devour all the people round about, on the right hand and on the left: and Jerusalem shall be inhabited again in her own place, even in Jerusalem."   (verse 6)

We believe we can see in Samson's use of these things the hand of God at work. God is light. He is the supreme, all powerful God in whom is no darkness (1 John 1:5). The land was, and still is, His covenant land and Israel His covenant people. What Israel had failed to do in not driving out the Philistines, God was now showing them how to accomplish, through Samson. The flaming torches tied to the foxes were symbols of the hand of Yahweh and His power and judgement. As we see from Zechariah, God uses the same symbology to describe His work in the future.

The Lord, through Samson, brought devastation to the Philistine economy; an act that was to lead to two further blows being inflicted on Israel's enemy by God's strong man in his work of beginning to deliver his people.

Blameless and shining as lights

In our lives now, as believers in the Lord Jesus Christ, we are not meant to be instruments for God's judgement on others as Samson was. In the age to come, however, those who are accepted by our Lord at his return are promised the role of kings and priests and will be given power to rule, and help the Lord to judge the world in righteousness.

What though of the present? There is an interesting link in the Epistle to the Philippians with Samson declaring that he would be blameless, and then using torches to bring judgement on the Philistines. The words of Paul are found in chapter 2:

> "Wherefore, my beloved, as ye have always obeyed, not as in my presence only, but now much more in my absence, work out your own salvation with fear and trembling. For it is God which worketh in you both to will and to do of his good pleasure. Do all things without murmurings and disputings: *that ye may be blameless* and harmless, the sons of God, without rebuke, in the midst of a crooked and perverse nation, *among whom ye shine as lights in the world; holding forth the word of life*; that I may rejoice in the day of Christ, that I have not run in vain, neither laboured in vain."

(Philippians 2:12-16)

God was not able to work through His people Israel in the time of the Judges. They constantly did evil and turned from Him. They were the children of those who had murmured and complained during the journey from Egypt and so had perished in the wilderness. The Lord did, however, work with, and through, His chosen judges who were raised up as saviours. Such was the man Samson.

But although we cannot directly compare ourselves with Samson and the events recorded in the early verses of Judges 15, we can take the exhortation of Paul to ourselves. God can work in our lives to do His good pleasure if we have the right will, or disposition, and prayerfully seek to work out our salvation with fear and trembling. We too must be blameless and harmless and shine, as Samson did, as lights in this dark, crooked and perverse world until our Lord returns.

Hip and thigh

As a result of Samson destroying the Philistines' harvest, they in turn retaliate and his father-in-law the Timnite, and his unfaithful "wife", lose their lives. The life she had tried to save by betraying him in relation to the riddle was in the end lost anyway (Judges 15:4-6).

This act of burning his wife caused Samson to speak of avenging the Philistines and then ceasing (verse 7). These two verses, 7 and 8, are perhaps two of the most difficult verses in the Samson record to expound; but the record does not say God condemned His saviour's actions. In fact, what Samson does actually becomes part of this whole situation of judgement on Israel's enemy, which is being controlled by the Lord. As we see from verse 14 it was to lead to "the Spirit of the LORD" coming mightily upon Samson once again. If Samson's strength came from God, and not his own physical prowess, then again it was through the Spirit of the Lord that he was being used as part of the deliverance of God's people from the Philistine domination. Samson says that after he has been avenged he will cease. This reads as if Samson had no more intention of fighting the Philistines after what he did in smiting them "hip and thigh", even though he knew of God's purpose with him. Whatever he meant at that moment in time, it didn't happen then. As the rest of the chapter shows us, God's providential work with Samson was not finished.

So Samson smote the Philistines "hip and[4] thigh with a great slaughter". This expression is thought to describe hand-to-hand combat in wrestling. Compare how Samson with the Spirit

---

4   Strong: "above, over, upon, or against." Hebrew, 'leg upon thigh'.

of God overcame the lion with his bare hands (14:6). The word "hip" means according to Strong, "from a root word meaning, the (lower) leg (as a runner)". Its use in scripture has two meanings. In relation to man it refers to the lower leg, the calf; but in reference to animals it refers to the thigh or upper leg as in the case of the portion of the sacrifices eaten by the priests. One interesting use in relation to man is in Psalm 147:

> "He delighteth not in the strength of the horse: he taketh not pleasure in the *legs* of a man. The LORD taketh pleasure in them that fear him, in those that hope in his mercy."
>
> (verses 10,11)

In the context here we see the reference has to do with the strength of man which God takes no pleasure in compared to those who fear Him and hope in His mercy. The Hebrew word for "thigh" is the word which Strong gives as, "from an unused root meaning to be soft; the thigh (from its fleshy softness); by euphemism the generative parts; figuratively, a shank, flank, side". The *TWOT* has the following comments in its definition of the word: "The thigh stands for man's foundation (e.g., 'the place of girding on the sword' (Judges 3:16,21) and for the source of life. Thus the hand placed under the thigh affirmed the strongest oath, especially during the patriarchal age (Genesis 24:9) ... No wonder the angel in his wrestling match with Jacob at Peniel smote Jacob's thigh. He showed his superior strength, and he indicated that the very basis of Jacob's life was altered, further signified by the change of his name ... (Genesis 32:25,31)."

These definitions, and usages, seem to suggest that man's strength and prowess, and the part of the body where he would carry his weapons, cannot compete with the strength that comes from God and the power of His Spirit; of which Jacob was left with a reminder for the rest of his life.

Whatever this expression "hip and thigh" means, the key point is that it was "a great slaughter" and resulted in them wanting to capture the man they later described as their enemy, who had destroyed their country and slew many of them (Judges

16:24). Again this supports the whole purpose of Samson's birth and the mission God had for him. If Samson was not naturally physically strong how did he accomplish this great slaughter without the Spirit of God working in him?

The attempt to capture the destroyer of their country and the outcome of their efforts will be the subject of the next chapter (page 77).

"Vengeance is mine, I will repay, saith the LORD"

Before we leave these incidents recorded in the early verses of Judges 15 there is an important lesson for us to remember.

Although the Almighty does not condemn Samson for his actions against the Philistines, which we have suggested are part of the "occasion" against Israel's enemy that God was orchestrating through His chosen saviour, we must remember that for us vengeance and retaliation are not things we are to take into our own hands. In fact under the Law of Moses this was forbidden against a fellow Israelite:

> "Thou shalt not avenge, nor bear any grudge against the children of thy people, but thou shalt love thy neighbour as thyself: I am the LORD."   (Leviticus 19:18)

For the disciple of the Lord there are clear commands to observe. Just consider a few of the New Testament passages that teach us how we should act:

> "Dearly beloved, avenge not yourselves, but rather give place unto wrath: for it is written, Vengeance is mine; I will repay, saith the Lord. Therefore if thine enemy hunger, feed him; if he thirst, give him drink: for in so doing thou shalt heap coals of fire on his head. Be not overcome of evil, but overcome evil with good."   (Romans 12:19-21)

> "Ye have heard that it hath been said, An eye for an eye, and a tooth for a tooth: but I say unto you, That ye resist not evil: but whosoever shall smite thee on thy right cheek, turn to him the other also."   (Matthew 5:38,39)

We are even told to love our enemies and those who persecute us (Matthew 6:44).

To live and act as we are exhorted in these passages takes great faith and courage. We must trust in our Heavenly Father at all times knowing that He knows best and that He will be faithful to His word: "Vengeance is mine, I will repay, saith the Lord."

One man will chase a thousand

Betrayal, victory and prayer

S AMSON, having smote the Philistines "hip and thigh with a great slaughter", retreated to the top (or cleft) of the rock Etam[1] (Judges 15:7,8).

The Hebrew word for "rock"[2] is used in various contexts including usage by the psalmist David who looked on the Lord as his "Rock", his place of safety and security (Psalm 18:2). In His purpose with Samson God had so far been His saviour's Rock just as He was later to be David's. Samson, in faith, had put his trust in the Lord and the Spirit of the Lord had come mightily upon him.

The same stability that can only be found in the Almighty God of Israel is an exhortation that shouts out for us to take to ourselves. He is the One who can be our fortress and our strong salvation. Compare the words of Psalm 71:3 which no doubt would be similar to the thoughts of Samson as a man of faith and from which we too must learn:

> "Be thou my strong habitation, whereunto I may continually resort: thou hast given commandment to save me; for thou art my rock and my fortress."[3]

---

1   According to Strong, 'Etam' means 'hawk ground'. It comes from the root word meaning 'bird of prey and to swoop down upon'.

2   Strong: "from an unused root meaning to be lofty; a craggy rock, literally or figuratively (a fortress)."

3   This Psalm, although not titled, is thought to be a Psalm of David. It is also Messianic, especially in relation to the Lord in Gethsemane. Reading it through,

We are not told why Samson went to this particular rock rather than returning to his home, but it may be because it appears to be in the portion of the land allotted to Judah. There is a place called Etam[4] near Bethlehem, part of the inheritance of Judah but allotted to the Simeonites (1 Chronicles 4:32). It was later fortified by Rehoboam (2 Chronicles 11:6). Whether or not the rock Etam was near the village, the tribe of Judah itself had figured prominently in the task of overcoming the land right at the start of the book of Judges. Part of their initial work of fighting against the inhabitants of the land was to take the city of Gaza and Ashkelon – the very two Philistine cities with which Samson was involved (Judges 1:18). Now towards the end of the period of the Judges, instead of fighting the Philistines, they showed fear and utter faithlessness in the Lord their God. They forsook the Lord when they saw the enemy spread out before them. They were selfish and apathetic, and had submitted to the Philistines' rulership over them. Note that the word "rulers" is the same as the word "dominion" in chapter 14:4.

The record does not tell us the degree to which Samson's great slaughter affected the Philistines: but the result was they sent at least a thousand men and pitched, or encamped, in Lehi in Judah with the intention to bind Samson (15:9,10). It also says they "spread themselves". The Hebrew word for "spread" occurs forty times in the Old Testament, half of which carry the idea of 'forsake'. But it is also used in the context of an army spreading itself out in the battlefield. It is interesting that this word is almost exclusively used in this way of the Philistines (cf. 1 Samuel 4:2; 2 Samuel 5:18,22). The Philistines said they had come to bind Samson and to do to him as he had done to them. This word "bind" is used fifteen times in relation to Samson; five times in Judges 15 and ten in chapter 16. In each case Samson, with his God-given strength, is able to break his bonds except on

---

think how much of it could describe Samson.

4　　Cf. comments in *The Book of Judges* – Cambridge Bible for Schools and Colleges, page 165.

the last occasion when the Lord had departed from him, and he was then bound with fetters of brass.

The men of Judah, after having been told why the Philistines had come, sent three thousand of their own men to Samson. It is possible, if there were only a thousand Philistines in their army that the men of Judah outnumbered them three to one: yet because they lacked faith, they never lifted a finger to help Samson. Instead they went to Samson and told him they had come to hand him over to the enemy (verse 11)! They only thought of themselves: "What is this that *thou hast done unto us*?" Instead of looking to Samson's example of faith and courage in destroying the Philistines' harvest and slaughtering many of them, the men of Judah were willing to betray their own separation to God, as His chosen people, for the price of peace: and so were ready to hand over to their enemy the one born and separated to be their saviour. Their rejection of God's chosen deliverer was in fact a rejection of God Himself. Samson, however, meekly agreed to be bound fast[5] and taken by them as long as they promised not to kill him themselves (verses 12,13). This was again an act of faith on Samson's part; for he had to trust in the Lord that He would be with him and protect him so he could complete his work as Israel's God-given judge and saviour.

The reaction of the Philistine men at the sight of Samson bound, and ready to be handed over to them, was to shout against him. As far as they were concerned their enemy was now at their mercy. They "shouted"[6] with a cry of victory. Incidentally, this is the same Hebrew word used in 1 Samuel 4:5 when Israel shouted at the sight of the Ark of God being brought onto the battlefield which they presumed would bring them victory against the Philistine enemy. But it didn't because God had other plans in His foreknowledge and purpose. And so it was to be in

---

5   The Hebrew has "bind, bind" – a double emphasis.

6   Strong: "to mar especially by breaking; figuratively, to split the ears with sound, i.e., shout for alarm or joy."

this incident with Samson. This time it was the Philistines who were unprepared for what happened next, for God was to act on behalf of His saviour.

As Samson was brought bound to the joyful Philistines at Lehi we are told, "the Spirit of the LORD came mightily upon him" (verse 14). God's work with His saviour hadn't ceased in contrast to Samson's words in verse 7. And so with the strength received from God, his cords were broken, and with a new, or moist, jawbone of an ass he slew one thousand of the enemy (verses 14-16). Was Samson encouraged by the exploits of Shamgar (Judges 3:31)? Samson had come from the hawk ground and now, as it were, swoops down on the Philistines suddenly like a bird of prey. Note again however, that by using this moist jawbone, Samson, if under a true Nazarite vow, would once more be rendered unclean and the vow forfeited. But as we have seen there was no vow to break.

The jawbone of an ass

Was it also just coincidence that Samson, when released from his bonds by the strength received through the Spirit of God coming upon him, should happen to reach out and find *the jawbone of an ass* by which he could slay the Philistines? Let us remember again the principle of the book of Judges that God raised up Israel's saviours and was with them in their work for Him.

The ass was an unclean animal, a beast of burden. When God had redeemed the children of Israel from Egypt He had singled out the ass when teaching them the principle of the redemption of the firstborn:

"And it shall be when the LORD shall bring thee into the land of the Canaanites, as he sware unto thee and to thy fathers, and shall give it thee, that thou shalt set apart unto the LORD all that openeth the matrix and every firstling that cometh of a beast which thou hast; the males shall be the LORD's. And every firstling of an *ass* thou shalt redeem with a lamb; and if thou wilt not redeem it, then thou shalt break his neck:

and all the firstborn of man among thy children shalt thou redeem. And it shall be when thy son asketh thee in time to come, saying, What is this? that thou shalt say unto him, *By strength of hand the* LORD *brought us out from Egypt*, from the house of bondage: and it came to pass, when Pharaoh would hardly let us go, that the LORD slew all the firstborn in the land of Egypt, both the firstborn of man, and the firstborn of beast: therefore I sacrifice to the LORD all that openeth the matrix, being males; but all the firstborn of my children I redeem. And it shall be for a token upon thine hand, and for frontlets between thine eyes: *for by strength of hand the* LORD *brought us forth out of Egypt*." (Exodus 13:11-16)

We see first then that the ass is a representation of God's chosen people[7] who had been beasts of burden to the Egyptians, and unclean before God. But the firstling of the ass could be redeemed, just like the firstborn of Israel, with the sacrifice of a lamb or kid of the goats at the Passover. These words were spoken to the people in the context, not only of redemption, but also of being a reminder in time to come that "by strength of hand the LORD brought us out from Egypt, from the house of bondage".

Now, in the time of the Judges, Israel was again in bondage. The Lord had delivered them into the hand of the Philistines. But even more tragic was the fact that they had delivered their God-given saviour, a firstborn son, representative of God's people at large, bound, to their enemy. Despite their actions God was with Samson, as He would be with them if only they served Him faithfully and turned to Him for help.

Another parable for Israel

Here in Samson's use of the jawbone of the ass was to be another dramatic parable for Israel. The ass represented them as it did Israel at the time of the Exodus. When God delivered His firstborn from Egypt He did it by the strength of His hand. Now

---

7   Remember the passage in Jeremiah 2:23,24 which we referred to earlier: see chapter 4 (page 51).

He was using that same power in the firstborn son of Manoah to begin to deliver Israel from the Philistines. Samson's use of the jawbone of the ass surely taught Israel that human nature, sinful, weak and unclean as it was, could, with God's strength, overcome the enemy.

Israel spiritually dead

At that time God's people were dead spiritually. They were like the jawbone of the ass, useless and unable to save themselves from those who had dominion over them. Unlike on previous occasions, this time they had failed to use their own jawbones, their mouths, to cry out to God for help because of the oppression they suffered. Their voices were silent, dead to prayer and supplication and an acknowledgement of their sins. But Samson's use of the jawbone illustrated that even weak, sinful, and "dead" people, when energised by the Spirit of God, can be a force to be reckoned with. As the Lord later illustrated through the prophet Ezekiel, even a valley of dry bones, representative of the house of Israel, can be brought together by the Spirit of God and turned into an "exceeding great army" (Ezekiel 37:1-14). God, through His grace and power, can use weak things to overcome the strong, as scripture teaches elsewhere (1 Corinthians 1:27; 2 Corinthians 12:9; Philippians 4:13; Hebrews 11:34).

These New Testament passages provide powerful exhortations for all God's servants.

Another link to Israel

There is however another link between the jawbone and Israel when we consider the word "new". The only other occasion we find the original word used is right at the beginning of the prophecy of Isaiah when God condemns His people for once again provoking Him with their sins. In the Lord's graphic description of His people in the days of Uzziah, Jotham, Ahaz and Hezekiah, the same Hebrew word is used of them. Note also that again Israel is compared to an ass:

"Hear, O heavens, and give ear, O earth: for the LORD hath spoken, I have nourished and brought up children, and they have rebelled against me. The ox knoweth his owner, and the *ass* his master's crib: but Israel doth not know, my people doth not consider. Ah sinful nation, a people laden with iniquity, a seed of evildoers, children that are corrupters: they have forsaken the LORD, they have provoked the Holy One of Israel unto anger, they are gone away backward. Why should ye be stricken any more? ye will revolt more and more: the whole head is sick, and the whole heart faint. From the sole of the foot even unto the head there is no soundness in it; but wounds, and bruises, and *putrifying*[8] sores: they have not been closed, neither bound up, neither mollified with ointment."   (Isaiah 1:2-6)

These words echo the state of God's people in the days of the Judges. At that time also they had forsaken the Lord; and instead of delivering Samson to the Philistines the men of Judah should have turned to the Lord in faith and helped God's chosen saviour in his work of deliverance from their enemy. They had done it in the past but failed to attempt to do it in the days of Samson. They failed to learn the lessons God taught them through Joshua and which He was teaching them once again through the deliverer He had raised up:

"Be ye therefore very courageous to keep and to do all that is written in the book of the law of Moses, that ye turn not aside therefrom to the right hand or to the left; that ye come not among these nations, these that remain among you; neither make mention of the name of their gods, nor cause to swear by them, neither serve them, nor bow yourselves unto them: but cleave unto the LORD your God, as ye have done unto this day. For the LORD hath driven out from before you great nations and strong: but as for you, no man hath been able to stand before you unto this day. *One man of you shall chase a thousand: for the LORD your God, he it is that fighteth for*

---

8   This is the same Hebrew word as "new" in Judges 15:15.

you, as he hath promised you. Take good heed therefore unto yourselves, that ye love the LORD your God."

(Joshua 23:6-11)

Samson was such a man. He was, at that time, living proof that God was faithful to His word. Samson not only chased a thousand Philistines but slew them through the Spirit of the Lord coming mightily upon him.

Strong in the Lord

We too are not alone in our battle against sin if we have faith in the One who has blessed us. God is our strong salvation through Jesus Christ His Son. We can do all things with God's strength if it is His will. We must not put our trust in man in whom there is no help or salvation (Psalm 146:3).

When life gets difficult it is so easy to compromise our faith, as did Israel in the days of Samson. They were prepared to submit to their enemy, the Philistines, and not lift a finger to help themselves or their God-provided saviour. They failed to learn the lessons provided by the Lord through His appointed judge.

We, however, must learn and believe that one man or woman with God is a majority. "What shall we then say to these things? If God be for us, who can be against us?" (Romans 8:31). We have to "be strong in the Lord, and in the power of His might". Daily we must "put on the whole armour of God", including prayer[9] (Ephesians 6:10-18). If we have committed ourselves to being God's servants we must try to do His will; always fighting the fight of faith, and holding forth the word of life as shining lights in a dark age (Philippians 2:15,16).

With God on his side Samson, through faith, and Judges like Shamgar and Gideon before him, and David after him, could achieve great victories with only simple fighting instruments. They used what was in their hand to serve God. There is an

---

9   This is what God's people had failed to do in the time of Samson.

interesting contrast in the days of Saul when the people, like those in the days of Samson, failed to use what they had in their hand to fight the Philistines. Instead of using instruments similar to the one Shamgar used to slay six hundred Philistines, they went down to their enemy to have them sharpened so they could get on with their everyday work and lives (1 Samuel 13:19-23). They lacked faith. In contrast to Saul and the people, Jonathan, in 1 Samuel 14:6, displays the same quality of faith as men like Shamgar, Samson and David, when he said to the young man that carried his armour, "the LORD will work for us: for there no restraint to the LORD to save by many or by few". As a result of this display of faith the Philistine garrison was overcome.

The Apostle Paul seems to pick up this contrast and provide exhortation for believers in Christ in his inspired words to the Romans:

> "Neither yield ye your members as instruments of unrighteousness unto sin: but yield yourselves unto God, as those that are alive from the dead, and your members as instruments of righteousness unto God."   (Romans 6:13)

The word "yield" means 'present', and the word "instrument" means 'armour or weapons'.

We are being exhorted to use the members of our body as weapons in God's service; to use what we have individually to do His work and fight against our enemy "Sin". We have a daily choice to make: serve God with all we have, or serve Sin. We must follow the example of men like Samson and "fight the good fight of faith" (1 Timothy 6:12).

Jesus rides on an ass

Let us just pause for a moment in our studies of Samson to reflect on the Lord Jesus Christ. As we will show at the end of our studies, Samson was a type of the Lord in so many ways. Both, of course, were God-given saviours. Concerning the Lord's work of salvation we read in the prophecy of Zechariah 9 these words:

"Rejoice greatly, O daughter of Zion; shout, O daughter of Jerusalem: behold, thy King cometh unto thee: he is just, and having salvation; lowly, and riding upon an ass, and upon a colt the foal of an ass."   (verse 9)

Luke records in chapter 19 these words of the Lord:

"... Go ye into the village over against you; in the which at your entering ye shall find a colt tied, whereon yet never man sat: loose him, and bring him hither."   (verse 30)

To accomplish his work of salvation, the Lord Jesus, the antitype of the judges, rode an untamed ass – one on which no man had sat, into Jerusalem. The ass was a type of man – the flesh untamed. Jesus took control of the ass, as he did with the flesh. To be God's promised king, the Messiah, he had first to overcome the flesh – overcome his own nature which he shared with us. But sharing our nature meant he had to die. However, through his sinless life, the grave could not hold him: and by God's mighty Spirit power he was raised from the dead to become a living saviour through whom others could be delivered.

"The God of Salvation"

Having individually slain the enemy, without the help of his own people, Samson then recounts (to the men of Judah) what he had achieved:

"And Samson said, With the jawbone of an ass, heaps upon heaps, with the jaw of an ass have I slain a thousand men."
                                                    (Judges 15:16)

The Hebrew word for "heaps" only occurs here and comes from a root word meaning 'to boil up, ferment, to glow, to smear with pitch'. These men of Judah had witnessed the power of God in one man coming to the boil as Samson slew so many of their enemies.

But why did Samson emphasise this? Was it a selfish idle boast? Surely it was said in contrast to the words of his countrymen in verse 11: "Knowest thou not that the Philistines are rulers over us?" Samson's words, as we have already seen, were an echo of the words of Joshua to Israel in Joshua 23:10: "One man of you shall chase a thousand: for the LORD your God, he it is that fighteth for you, as he hath promised you." This was a call to the people to be like him, to go out against the enemy trusting in the Lord.

Samson then casts the jawbone away and calls that place "Ramath-lehi" – "the height of a jawbone" (verse 17). Was this another sign to the men of Judah who had witnessed the slaughter, but had not lifted a finger to help, that they likewise would be cast away by the Lord if they failed to put their trust in Him? Israel, represented by the jawbone, could have reached spiritual heights in their conquest of the land if only they had served the Lord, and not turned to the gods of the nations they should have destroyed. Interestingly the only other occurrences of 'Ramath'[10] are in Ezekiel 16 where in four verses (24,25,31,39) it is translated as "high place(s)" and refers to Jerusalem's idolatry and sins. Because of this the Lord did cast away His people for seventy years.

Samson's thirst

The result of their saviour's mighty victory over the Philistine army through God's Spirit coming upon him is that Samson becomes "sore athirst" (verse 18). Like all men and women he felt the weakness of the flesh. Although God's Spirit had come upon him to accomplish this great victory over Israel's enemy, his own strength was sapped in the process. Here was a test of his faith in the Lord. So he calls to the Almighty in prayer. He acknowledges that God has given him this "deliverance", or salvation. The Lord had given Samson to a barren woman to begin to deliver His people Israel from the Philistines. The power that had brought about his birth was the same power that had given him deliverance from the Philistine army that had come to take revenge upon him. The Almighty would surely not have brought His Spirit power upon Samson, to slay so many who sought revenge, if the events recorded earlier in the chapter had

10 Strong's no. 07413.

been the actions of a man who only sought his own satisfaction and lust without faith in the One who had provided him as a saviour. But God did, and Samson, in faith, recognised He had given him this great deliverance.

This is the first occasion this Hebrew word translated "deliverance" is used in scripture; and it is used by the man who is described by so many as a wayward and lustful man. But that we are suggesting is not the character of Samson. This prayer displays a man of faith who recognises the power of Almighty God in his life and work. In the remaining thirty-three occasions this word is used in the Old Testament at least thirty are in the context of, or mainly a direct reference to, God being "the God of salvation" (cf. Psalm 38:22; 51:14; Isaiah 46:13; Jeremiah 3:23; Lamentations 3:26). This is the same Hebrew word used by Jonathan of the salvation David brought for Israel as a result of slaying Goliath (1 Samuel 19:5). The root word for "deliverance" is the one used in Judges 2:

> "And when the LORD raised them up judges then the LORD was with the judge and *delivered* them out of the hand of their enemies all the days of the judge." (verse 18; see also verse 16)

It is also used in chapter 13:5 of Samson beginning to deliver, or save, his people. This root word was used by David himself to Goliath in 1 Samuel 17:47. In contrast the scripture exhortation is that we are not to put our trust in the "salvation", or "help",[11] of men (Psalm 146:3). So Samson acknowledges that God has given him this great deliverance. Note also the word "great" is the same as used of the "great slaughter" Samson accomplished in Judges 15:8, and of his "great strength" in 16:5,6,15.

The Lord's servant

In his prayer to God Samson calls himself the Lord's "servant" (Judges 15:18). He is the only judge who calls himself, or is called, the Lord's servant apart from the boy Samuel when he

---

11   The same Hebrew word.

answered God's call in the tabernacle at Shiloh (1 Samuel 3:9). This is the word God used of Abraham, Moses, Joshua, Caleb and David when He called them "My servant". Samson therefore acknowledged his call to serve the Lord and again demonstrated that he was a man of faith.

We too are the Lord's servants through God's grace. We have already quoted from Paul's words to the Romans in chapter 6 in relation to using what we have in our service to God rather than to Sin. Because of our association with the Lord Jesus Christ in the waters of baptism, having obeyed from the heart that form of doctrine which was delivered to us, we have been made free from sin and have become servants to righteousness and servants to God. What a tremendous privilege this is – a privilege that leads on to the hope of everlasting life.

A well of salvation

Samson's words "and now shall I die for thirst …?" are not the words of a faithless man complaining to God. Rather they are spoken in the context of his recognition that God was his strength. The Lord gave him power over the enemy; without it he was as weak as any other man. He was a man of like passions as we ourselves. He too experienced the frailties of the flesh that often test our faith. Was therefore God's work with him finished? Would he now fall into the hands of the uncircumcised Philistines as his work was only to *begin* to deliver Israel?[12] God's answer was to demonstrate to Samson that He truly was his strength and salvation; and that His servant was totally reliant on Him and so must serve Him in faith. Sadly it was when he forgot God that He departed from him and he did fall into the hands of the uncircumcised[13] enemy (Judges 16:21).

---

12 The words of Samson at the end of verse 18 again seem to support the view that he was not the man of strength he is so often portrayed as, and that without God working through him he was unable to perform the superhuman feats recorded of him.

13 Samson's use of this word to describe the Philistines echoes the words of his parents in chapter 14:3 and surely emphasises his true feelings about them. It

The Lord responds to Samson by providing him with water
and as a result "his spirit came again, and he revived" (verse 19). If
we remember that the place of Samson's victory with the jawbone
was called "Lehi" which means 'jawbone', then it makes more sense
that God split a hollow place in Lehi (the place of God's salvation)
for Samson to drink so that his spirit was revived. Comparing
other translations seems to support this interpretation.

The Hebrew word for "clave" is the same as the word
used to describe Yahweh's dividing of the Red Sea when Moses
stretched out his hand with the rod of God to enable Israel to
cross over (Exodus 14:16; Psalm 78:13). The same word is used
again in Psalm 78:15 when it records that the Lord "clave in the
rocks in the wilderness and gave them drink as out of the great
depths"; compare also Isaiah 48:21. What Samson, and Israel
before him, experienced was a foretaste of what the Almighty
will do in the kingdom age when the desert will blossom as a rose
(Isaiah 35:1-6).

So having been refreshed by Yahweh, Samson now calls
the place "Enhakkore": which means 'fountain of one calling',
or 'the well of him that called, or, cried'. He had called to God
who, in turn, had heard his prayer and provided living water for
His servant to drink. Compare the words God foretells would be
spoken of Him in Isaiah 12:

> "Behold, God is my salvation; I will trust, and not be afraid:
> for the LORD JEHOVAH is my strength and my song; he also is
> become my salvation. Therefore with joy shall ye draw water
> out of the wells of salvation."[14]   (Isaiah 12:2,3)

The water of life

In our fight against sin and the flesh there are going to be times
when we shall feel weary just as Samson did. Samson called on the

---

also provides evidence that Samson was not a lover of Philistine women as many
commentators propound if he described them as uncircumcised.

14 The Hebrew word for "salvation" is the same as the word for "deliverance" used by
Samson.

Lord; the One who is "the fountain of living waters" (Jeremiah 2:13; 17:13). But when we too become weary in our battles and perhaps feel we cannot go on, we, like Samson, must remember that only God through His Son provides the spiritual living water to refresh and sustain us in our work for Him. We need the daily intake of the water of life, from His word, to provide the spiritual refreshment to our weary minds.

Compare also Psalm 1. In the truest sense, the words of this Psalm can only refer to the Lord Jesus Christ. But we too, if we follow his example, can be encouraged with the promise of being blessed if we turn aside from the ways of the world and meditate in the Lord's law, His word, day and night as he did. In doing this we can be –

> "like a tree planted by the rivers of water, that bringeth forth his fruit in his season; his leaf also shall not wither; and whatsoever he doeth shall prosper."   (Psalm 1:3)

This Psalm not only reminds us of the living power of God's word to refresh and sustain us, but also that it will make us fruitful, and will prosper our way, as we seek to be faithful servants of the living God. As the Master said to the woman of Samaria, "whosoever drinketh of the water that I shall give him shall never thirst; but the water that I shall give him shall be in him a well of water springing up into everlasting life" (John 4:14). Remember also the words in Isaiah 55:1, and the book of Revelation 21:6.

Samson judges for twenty years

Another important point to note is the fact that God chose to insert after these events that began in chapter 13 and culminated in Him providing refreshment for His servant, the information that Samson "judged Israel in the days of the Philistines twenty years" (Judges 15:20). This is the only occasion in Judges where it says that a God-provided saviour judges during the time of the oppressor's dominion. In Samson's case this supports the role he was born to fulfil – only to *begin* to deliver Israel – and so must mean he judged during those forty years they dominated God's people. But note that in chapter 16:31 God chooses to repeat the statement at the end of Samson's life.

Why are we told this here in chapter 15 and again at the end of his life? One possible suggestion is that after slaying one thousand Philistines, there was a period of up to twenty years when the Philistines were less active due to their decimated land and army and their fear of *God's strong man of Israel* – a time in which Samson judged that area of Israel: i.e., Judah and the camp of Dan. We have already noted that the recorded incidents of his life would only account for *a small percentage* of the twenty years he judged.

What happened during the rest of that period of time is not revealed. The inspired record does not give us any more information about Samson's life, or achievements, during that time apart from the last few incidents recorded in chapter 16. If there was a period of rest during the latter half of the Philistine oppression of forty years then this would allow Samuel living in Ramah, in the middle of the land, to be established as a prophet of the Lord and begin his influence upon the people. As we know already from Judges 2:18, the Lord was with the judges He raised up and this included Samson. We are not told what influence Samson had on his fellow countrymen during that time. There is no record of him leading them into battle as did some of the other judges God raised up. As we have already suggested, he could also have been the buffer between the Philistines and the Ark of God at Kirjath-jearim.

It would appear from 1 Samuel 7:3,4 and Judges 2:13 that all through the period of the judges the majority of God's people still worshipped Baalim and Ashtaroth. There is no record of the people heeding the example of Samson and the words he spoke in Judges 15:16, which echoed the words of Joshua in Joshua 23:10. Neither does the record tell us of any other situations in which Samson attacked or slew other Philistines, or displayed extraordinary feats of strength. There is certainly nothing in the record to suggest Samson spent these twenty years in lustful, self-seeking ways. On the contrary, the record says he "judged Israel" and as we have just emphasised again, the Lord would have been with him.

This therefore poses the question, did the final two incidents in Judges 16 come at the end of his twenty years of judgeship? The way the record informs us that he judged for twenty years suggests they did. Compare the beginning of chapter 16:1, "*Then* went Samson to Gaza ..." This seems to suggest it was after his time of judging Israel that he decides to go to Gaza. Why though did Samson go there?

We shall consider this in the next chapter (page 95).

7 |

Possessing the gate of his enemies

Samson goes to Gaza – why?

W
HY, at the end of twenty years judging his people, did Samson go to Gaza? This was the furthest city of the lords of the Philistines from where he lived – a distance of over thirty-five miles. First compare two passages of scripture:

> "Then *went* Samson to Gaza, and saw there *an harlot* [Hebrew means, 'harlot woman'], and *went in* unto her. *And it was told the Gazites, saying, Samson is come hither.* And they compassed him in, and laid wait for him all night in the gate of the city, and were quiet all the night, saying, In the morning, when it is day, we shall kill him. And Samson *lay* [same Hebrew word as 'lodged' in Joshua 2:1] till midnight, and arose at midnight, and took the doors of the gate of the city, and the two posts, and went away with them, bar and all, and put them upon his shoulders, and carried them up to the top of an hill that is before Hebron."   (Judges 16:1-3)

If we read this passage on its own we might assume at first, as many have, that Samson, having seen this woman, desired a sexual encounter with her. We have to acknowledge that the phrase "he went in unto her" is used elsewhere of the sexual relationship of man and woman.

However, is this really what this section of the record is all about?

If we compare this incident of Samson with a previous one recorded in the book of Joshua we can perhaps view it from a different perspective:

"And Joshua the son of Nun sent out of Shittim two men to spy secretly, saying, Go view the land, even Jericho. And they *went, and came into an harlot's house* [Hebrew means 'harlot woman'], named Rahab, and *lodged* there. *And it was told the king of Jericho, saying, Behold, there came men in hither to night of the children of Israel* to search out the country. And the king of Jericho sent unto Rahab, saying, Bring forth the men that are come to thee, which are entered into thine house: for they be come to search out all the country."   (Joshua 2:1-3)

Note the comparisons between these two passages:

Samson	Two spies
Went (walked)	**Went (walked)**
Harlot	**Harlot**
Lay (same Hebrew word as lodged)	**Lodged**
Come	*Came*
The men of Gaza are told	The king of Jericho is told

The words in bold (or bold italics) above are the same in Hebrew (or teach us the same ideas).

Let us note what the record *does not* say. It doesn't say he went to Gaza to seek a harlot. It says he "went" or 'walked' there and then "saw" a "harlot". We know the reason why the spies were sent to Jericho. Their purpose was to spy and view the land, and Jericho, in preparation for overcoming the land of the Amorites and bringing upon them God's judgements. Jericho, their strongest city, and its people were to be the first to be overcome, and then the rest of the inhabitants of the land were to follow.[1] So what of Samson? Why did he go a distance of over thirty-five miles to the city of Gaza? Did he go to satisfy the lust of the flesh? Surely he could have found a harlot much closer to the camp of Dan, if that was his purpose, rather than travel deep into Philistine territory and so in the process put himself in danger. Or did he go in faith, to fulfil the purpose of God, to bring judgement on the Philistine city whose name happens to mean 'strength'? If the motive was purely the satisfaction of the flesh, why did God then give him the strength he needed to inflict an embarrassing blow to the city, its lords and inhabitants; and in the process, possibly slay those who lay in wait for him, some of which may have been giants? Also, why at midnight?

If our proposition regarding where the record of Samson fits into the historical record is correct, then it's interesting to think of these two passages concerning going in to a harlot as bookends to the period of the children of Israel's history when they should have conquered the land. Joshua began the work and during the time of the judges the tribes should have completed it. Both visits result in the destruction of the defences of the cities involved. In the case of Jericho the whole of the city's wall fell down, but here in Judges 16 the doors and posts of the gate of the city are taken away by Samson.

Samson's actions would seem to be another parable, and should have taught Israel that, with God's strength, they could overcome the strength of their enemies. Gaza was a significant city of the Philistines. It comes from root words meaning 'strong, vehement, harsh, to be stout'. The Philistines were the first on the list of nations left unconquered to prove Israel's faithfulness to Yahweh their God (Judges 3:1-4). Gaza is the first of the cities of the lords of the Philistines listed in Joshua 13:3. It was also the first of the Philistine cities to be taken by Judah (cf. Judges 1:18); but later must have been allowed to be occupied again by the Philistines. Note too, that in the context of Judges 1:18,

---

1   According to the providential hand of God the spies also went to the house of the harlot Rahab because she and her family were to be saved.

verse 20 tells us of Hebron, Caleb and the sons of Anak. Compare also Joshua 11:22: "There was none of the Anakims (giants) left in the land of the children of Israel: only in Gaza, in Gath, and in Ashdod, there remained." Surely these pieces of information put together tell something more about Samson's reason for going to Gaza and it was nothing to do with the lust of the flesh.

Midnight

While God's chosen saviour "lay" or lodged (it's the same Hebrew word as in Joshua 2) in the harlot's house, the Philistines "compassed" or surrounded Samson,[2] lying in wait for him in the gate of the city and devising a plan to take him in the morning. Notice it says the Philistines were "quiet all the night". The Hebrew word for "quiet" according to Strong is the same as "plowed" that we considered in relation to the riddle Samson gave to his thirty companions (Judges 14:18). Here in this context we can imagine the quiet evil plans they had devised to bring about the capture and eventual death of their enemy. But whatever their intentions in order to accomplish this, they were thwarted because Samson made his move at "midnight". Why at midnight? Did he remember the judgement God brought on Egypt at midnight – the time when the Lord killed all the firstborn of the Egyptians and saved the firstborn of the children of Israel (Exodus 12:29)? Was this in Samson's mind when he strikes a blow against his enemy at midnight? He too was a firstborn son. Compare the words of the Psalmist in Psalm 119:62: "At midnight I will rise to give thanks unto thee because of thy righteous judgments." God through Samson was bringing righteous judgement on the city of Gaza.

Possessing the gate of the enemy

Having risen at midnight, Samson, with what must have been God-given strength, uproots the gate posts and doors of the

---

2   The same word is used for Israel compassing Jericho – Joshua 6.

city and carries them across country to Hebron, a city some forty miles to the east of Gaza. How this was possible is beyond our comprehension. But with God all things are possible. If the Lord was at work with His servant in bringing judgement on this Philistine city, as we truly believe to be the case, then there could have been a band of unseen angels assisting God's strong man of Israel. God's Spirit power is beyond measure and our understanding. But what of those who were waiting and scheming to take him? Did he first of all kill them: some of whom were possibly Anakims? Or did God cause a deep sleep to come upon them while Samson removed the doors and posts? Without either of these actions being taken Samson would have been frustrated in his purpose – but he wasn't. There is no mention of him being opposed in his actions.

The city of Hebron lies east of Gaza; as he approached the sun would be rising in the east, heralding a new day. Samson's name, as we have seen, means 'sunlight'. Here surely was a lesson for Israel. They had been commanded by God to go into the land and to possess the gate of their enemies as Samson did literally. And if they did – if they followed Samson's example – then a new day, a day of light, would arise for them and take them out of the darkness of the Philistine domination.

If we acknowledge that Samson was a man of faith, there is a deeper meaning as to why he takes the doors of the gate of Gaza to "a hill (mountain, RV) that is before Hebron".

The name Hebron means 'seat of association or alliance'. It was the place where Abraham and his family were buried. It was therefore associated with the promises God had made to the fathers. In fact it was to Hebron that Abraham went to dwell, and where he built an altar to the Lord, immediately after God made His promise to give him, and his seed, the land for ever.[3] According to Hebrews 11:39 Samson was among those who knew of the promise, but did not receive it in their lifetime.

---

3   Cf. Genesis 13:14-18.

Compare especially the final promise the Lord made to Abraham after he was willing to offer his only son Isaac. God said, "Thy seed shall possess the gate of his enemies" (Genesis 22:17). Samson did this literally and so became a type of the work of the Lord Jesus Christ – *the* seed of Abraham.[4] Surely the type is spoilt if we believe the basis of Samson's actions at Gaza was purely the lust of the flesh. But if Gaza is seen as a type of the strength of sin, then Samson went to the city for the purpose of bringing righteous judgement upon it through the strength of the Lord. The antitype, the Lord Jesus Christ, according to his Father's purpose, was to overcome the strength of sin and death through righteousness; not just in his own death and resurrection, but also, in the future, when he returns he will complete the work of possessing the gate of his enemies and fulfil the last and greatest promise the Lord made to Abraham.

Hebron was important for another reason because it was one of the appointed Cities of Refuge. The city of Hebron, and the mountain[5] were given to Caleb the faithful spy who himself, through faith in the Lord, slew the three sons of Anak (Joshua 14:10-15). Later in Joshua we are told the city was given to the Kohathites and the fields and surrounding villages were given to Caleb (Joshua 21:9-12).

We feel certain Samson would take courage, inspiration and faith from these things. *God's strength*, manifested in Samson, overcame *the gate* (the place of rulership and judgement) *of the Philistine city of strength*: Gaza. Surely this was meant to be a powerful lesson for Israel if only they would heed it. But more than that, for it was a type of Christ's work both at his first advent and when he returns again.

One other significant point about this incident is that we are told Samson carried the gates "upon his shoulders." If the gate represented the government of the city, then we are reminded of the words of Isaiah 9:

4   Cf. Galatians 3:16.
5   The same Hebrew word as "hill" in Judges 16:3.

"For unto us a child is born, unto us a son is given: and the government shall be upon his shoulder: and his name shall be called Wonderful, Counsellor, The mighty God, The everlasting Father, The Prince of Peace."   (verse 6)

In the kingdom age, when the Lord Jesus Christ has subdued all his enemies then truly *all governments* will be on his shoulders.[6] In all of this Samson truly was a type of Christ.

Judgement on all five cities of the lords of the Philistines

If Samson judged at the same time the Ark had been in the land of the Philistines and was then returned and kept for twenty years in Kirjath-jearim, then by the end of the forty years, of which Samson judged twenty years, God had brought judgement on *all five cities* of the lords of the Philistines (1 Samuel 6:17,18). Compare the following maps and chart.

---

6   Note the Hebrew word used in Isaiah, *shekem* – the neck – is different from that found in Judges 16:3, *katheph* – the shoulder (proper, i.e., upper end of the arm; as being the spot where the garments hang).

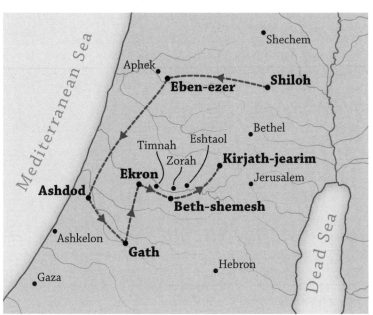

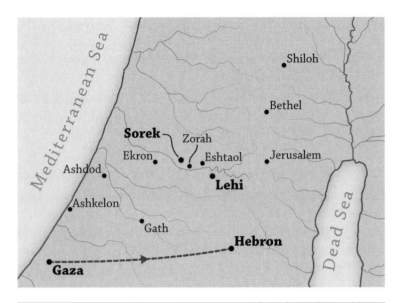

City	Judgement	Reference
Ashdod	Dagon their idol broken – destroyed and smitten with emerods, or tumours, by the hand of the Lord heavy upon them.	1 Samuel 5:1-8
Gath	The hand of the Lord was against them with a great destruction. Destroyed and smitten with emerods or tumours.	1 Samuel 5:8,9
Ekron	The hand of God was very heavy there. Destroyed and smitten with emerods or tumours.*	1 Samuel 5:10-12
Ashkelon	The spirit of the Lord came upon Samson and he slew thirty men and took a spoil.	Judges 14:19
Gaza	Samson removes the gates and carries them to Hebron. Samson is strengthened to destroy 3,000 Philistines as they mock him and sacrifice to their god Dagon.	Judges 16:3,23-30

* Cf. 2 Kings 1:1-16 where we learn that Baalzebub was the god of Ekron. Was this why the hand of God was *very* heavy there?

Further judgement

As far as the record of Samson is concerned, God's judgement on Gaza was soon to have a second phase. The taking of the gates of Gaza to Hebron brought judgement on the political aspect of the city. As we shall see in the penultimate chapter of our study, further judgement was to take place on the Philistines' religious system in Gaza as well.

Great and precious promises

Samson must have understood the promises to Abraham as Hebrews 11 makes clear; especially the final one in Genesis 22. These same promises must also remain in the forefronts of our minds. We too should always be focusing on the same "great and precious promises" as the inspired Apostle Peter describes them in 2 Peter 1:4. We need to learn from other faithful men and women of old who based their lives on the things God has revealed concerning His eternal purpose. These promises have been confirmed by the shedding of the Lord's blood when he died as the perfect sacrifice for sin (Romans 15:8; Hebrews 9:15). We, through faith and baptism into him, have become heirs to the promises God made of old (Galatians 3:26-29); promises which assure us that, in God's grace, we shall be partakers of the divine nature.

But faith is not enough. Peter, under inspiration goes on in his second epistle to exhort that we have to give all diligence, or speed, to *add*[7] to our faith (verse 5). Faith needs to lead us to apply the following qualities of virtue, knowledge, temperance, patience, godliness, brotherly kindness and charity (love) in our lives in Christ. Without these things we shall be unfruitful and blind spiritually. We shall also be short-sighted regarding the things that are afar off – the fulfilment of the great and precious promises to be fulfilled when our Lord returns, and forgetful of the meaning of the cleansing from our old sins by the Lord's sacrifice.

---

7   The Greek word means 'to furnish besides, that is to supply fully, aid or contribute'.

"Wherefore the rather, brethren, give diligence to make your calling and election sure: for if ye *do these things*, ye shall never fall: for so an entrance *shall be ministered unto you*[8] abundantly into the everlasting kingdom of our Lord and Saviour Jesus Christ."   (2 Peter 1:10,11)

This is the promise made to Samson as the inspired writer informs us in the epistle to the Hebrews; but it is also the promise we are assured of if we heed the apostle's exhortation, and give diligence to make our calling and election sure.

---

8   This phrase is the same as the Greek for "add".

Contrast Hebron and the men of Judah in relation to Samson and the time of David

- Samson was given, by the men of Judah, to the Philistines as a captive – they handed to the enemy the one God had chosen as their deliverer (Judges 15:11-13).
- Through Samson taking the gates of Gaza (the city of Philistine strength) to Hebron God showed that with faith in Him the men of Judah and all Israel could possess the gate of their enemies (16:3).
- In contrast, in the days of David the men of Judah came to David – who was in Hebron by direct revelation from God – and anointed him king (2 Samuel 2:1-4).
- David had proved in Judah's portion of the land that, with faith in God, the enemy (Goliath and the Philistines) could be overcome (cf. 1 Samuel 17:1,37,50-52).
- Had the "men of Judah" finally learned the lesson from Samson?

The tests of faith and love

Samson and Delilah

"And it came to pass afterward, that he loved a woman in the valley of Sorek, whose name was Delilah." (Judges 16:4)

SOMETIME after his exploits at Gaza Samson leaves Hebron, the place that means 'association or fellowship' and goes to seek association with a woman named Delilah in the valley of Sorek. We are clearly told he "loved" this woman. But who was she? There is no sound evidence in the record that she was a Philistine. Conversely there are reasons to believe she was an Israelitess.

Why Samson loved Delilah is not revealed. We are not told what brought about this love or what attracted him to her. We cannot conjecture that just because Samson is recorded as having had associations with two other women, which we have seen were part of God's purpose with him, that his love of Delilah was just a satisfaction of lustful desires.

'Delilah' means 'languishing, to be feeble'. The name comes from a primitive root: 'to slacken or be feeble; figuratively, to be oppressed'. This root word is used of Israel in Judges 6:6: "And Israel was greatly *impoverished* because of the Midianites; and the children of Israel cried unto the LORD."

Sorek in turn means 'a vine'. Again the root word is used of Israel (Isaiah 5:2; Jeremiah 2:21).

Delilah is "loved"[1] by Samson: the only one who it is said he loved. The woman of Timnath, who "pleased" Samson for the purpose God had at that time with the Philistines had spoken of love; but the record in Judges 14 does not say Samson loved her as it does about his love for Delilah. The same Hebrew word is used in Deuteronomy of man's love for God and His love for Israel (cf. Deuteronomy 6:5; 7:9,13; 10:12,15,18,19).

There is nothing in the record to prevent us believing that Delilah was one of God's chosen people. We are not told she was a Philistine. She lived in the territory given to the tribe of Dan and appears to have an Israelite name! We are told that the lords of the Philistines came to her. They didn't threaten her but offered her money. If she was one of their own people then surely they could have acted in a similar, threatening, way as with the woman of Timnath twenty years earlier. It would appear that because Samson loved her he also trusted her. Delilah herself used the term "*the Philistines* be upon you" during the occasions she sought to find out the source of Samson's strength. Contrast Judges 14:16 – "... thou hast put forth a riddle unto *the children of my people*, and hast not told it me ..." It would also appear that she understood the principle of being a *nâziyr*, or separate one, especially in relation to the cutting of the hair.

Putting all this information together, it poses the question, Is she there in the narrative as a type of Israel? Consider the points made in the following table.

Is Delilah a type of Israel?

Delilah	Israel
Lived in Sorek – 'vine'.	God's choice vine.
Her name means 'languishing or weak'.	Israel were languishing through sin.

---

1   Strong, "to have affection for – sexually or otherwise".

Delilah	Israel
She is the only one that it is said Samson loved.	Israel alone loved by Yahweh.
Lacked faith in God.	Lacked faith in God.
Willing to sell herself to the Philistines, betray her separation to God and Samson – the strength the Lord had provided to overcome the enemy.	Israel had willingly submitted to the Philistines and the surrounding nations and had betrayed the God of their salvation to worship Baalim and Ashtaroth.
Willing to give Samson to the enemy.	Willing to give Samson to the enemy.

So then it is possible to look at the story of Samson and Delilah as a parable with Delilah representing Israel. Compare again the details:

- There is no evidence to suggest she was a Philistine.
- Samson loved her.
- Her name means languishing – weak.
- She lived in the valley of Sorek ('a vine').
- She is enticed by the lust of the flesh to betray Samson – "The love of money is the root of all evil" (1 Timothy 6:10).

God's work with Samson is not yet complete

Before we consider what this incident with Delilah is revealing to us about the final stage of God's purpose with Samson, let us remember that up to this moment in time we have seen him as a man of faith who relied on his God and was driven by God's Spirit to begin to deliver Israel from the Philistine domination. Remember that the first thing the inspired narrative reveals to us about Samson in relation to God is that "the LORD blessed him" and "moved" him. Through Samson Yahweh was bringing about His final judgements on the cities of the lords of the Philistines. It is no wonder then that they are prepared to pay such a high price to know where his great strength lay and how they could bring retribution on him.

After twenty years of judging God's people His strong man had awaken out of sleep both symbolically and literally in the house of the harlot to bring about the start of God's judgement on Gaza. But that judgement was still to reach its completion and Samson himself was to be sacrificed in the process. The Almighty was still in control – His occasion against the Philistines was yet to reach its fulfilment through His chosen saviour. In all we have seen so far there has been no condemnation of Samson in the divine record.

We need to bear these thoughts in mind when we look at the incidents involving Samson, Delilah and the Philistines. Are we meant to see more than a man who on the surface appears to be mocking the woman he is said to love? If the Lord was the giver of Samson's strength how did he know God would enable him to free himself from the various bonds he said would make him as weak as other men. Can we really believe Samson was playing a game, at the centre of which, was the assumption that God's power would be given him just when he needed it? Compare the words of Jesus to the scribes who accused him of having the power of Beelzebub: "But he that shall blaspheme against the Holy Spirit hath never forgiveness, but is in danger of eternal damnation" (Mark 3:29). If Samson was misusing God's power surely he would be condemned, as the words of the Lord make clear.

But if we look at these incidents from a different point of view, rather than the one that presents Samson fooling around with the strength he receives from the Lord, then they can be seen to be tests of faith and love for both Delilah and for Samson himself.

Delilah's tests

Delilah was given, in effect, three tests to see if she would remain faithful to Samson: the symbol of God's strength, who could continue to deliver her, and Israel, from their enemy (Judges 16:6-14). But she rejects him the fourth time when Samson reveals to her his heart. Instead of remaining faithful to him she submits to the enemy's tempting offer. According to *BDB* the name "Philistine" means 'immigrant'. It comes from a root word meaning 'rolling or migratory'. Delilah allowed the Philistines' influence to 'immigrate' into her heart. There is no mention in the record of her love for Samson even though he loved her. In fact it would appear that her love was for the things of this life and so she betrays her God-given saviour for money. Compare the three times Pilate declared he found no fault in Jesus but still the people rejected their Saviour when for the fourth time he tries to release him.

As an aside: this incident supports our suggestion that Samson was not a man with bulging muscles – someone of a similar build to the giants found among the Philistine people. If he looked a man of great physique then surely it is unlikely the Philistine lords would want to know where his great strength came from. But they did, and it was Delilah who was tempted with a great sum of money to find the answer for them (verse 5).

When Samson reveals all his heart to her, and she understands the command he is under, Delilah has a last opportunity to put her trust in him and the God of her people, rather than in riches (verses 17-19). The choice was either God, manifested in Samson, or mammon, provided by the lords of the Philistines. Delilah chose riches and Samson was doomed. The meaning of her name describes what she was spiritually: weak and feeble. She was not prepared to be separate from the evil around her. She chose the things of the flesh over and above the things of the Spirit. She spurned the love of Samson for the love of money; the god of the Philistines above her own God, the God of Israel. Like the men of Judah in chapter 15 her rejection of Samson was, in effect, her rejection of Yahweh and so she typified the nation at large. Delilah "afflicted"[2] Samson; but did she also

---

2   The same Hebrew word is used of the Lord in Isaiah 53:4,7.

take pleasure in the mockery of Samson in Dagon's temple and so would have perished with those who Samson slew at his death?

Do these incidents have any significance?

If these incidents regarding Samson's strength were meant to be a test for Delilah, who represented Israel, as we have suggested, can we see in them any significance to the story of Samson and why God had raised him up? Let us examine the words used to describe them.

First test – seven green withs

"Seven" – this is significant for completion or perfection.

"Green" – the Hebrew word means 'new or fresh'. The word is used only six times; two of which are here in Judges 16. In three of the other occurrences it is used in the context of God having more strength or power than that which represents man's ability or strength. The only other occurrence describes the "moist" or "green" grapes forbidden under the Nazrarite law (Numbers 6:3).

"Withs" has the meaning of 'overhanging, excess, superiority, and remainder'. But here in Judges 16 it is translated "withs" or cord. Is its use here, in association with "seven" and "green", meant to give the idea of superior strength?

Samson, however, breaks these as the "thread of a tow". The Hebrew word for "tow" only occurs in one other place – Isaiah 1:31. There in the context it is the strong, or strength of man, that shall be as "tow", as a broken fibre of flax, when God brings judgement on those who transgress and forsake Him.

The overall lesson was that God's strength, His Spirit power given to Samson, was in fact more powerful than any strength man could provide to oppose or restrict it.

Second test – new ropes

The meaning of the words "new ropes" is exactly the same as those used in Judges 15:13 in relation to when the men of Judah bound Samson with "two new cords" and handed him over to the Philistines. This event would have been well known because Samson had, through the Spirit of God coming on him, not only broken the bonds that bound him but also slain one thousand of the Philistines with the jawbone of an ass. This had taken place some twenty years earlier after which Samson had been judging Israel.

It appears that neither Delilah, who represents Israel, or the Philistines, had learnt the lesson of all those years ago that the Lord God of Israel is the One who provides strength that is able to overcome the enemy. Samson had broken the new ropes previously when they had become as flax that is burnt in the fire: so why would they think he would be restrained by them this time?

Third test – seven locks of hair weaved into a web and pin

"Weavest" – This word is used in only two general contexts throughout the Old Testament. First it is used in relation to weaving the robe and coats of Aaron and his sons when the Tabernacle was constructed after the Exodus. All the other occasions it is used are in relation to false worship or behaviour which God will destroy, and so show that the might of man is powerless before Him.

"Web" – The word "web" has the meaning of 'spreading out; something expanded, the warp in a loom'. *BDB* and *TWOT* define it as 'web or web of unfinished stuff on a loom', giving the idea of something not completed.

"Pin" – The Hebrew word for "pin" is translated 'pin, peg, paddle or stake'. Again there seems to be two categories of use in the Old Testament. The first eight occurrences relate to the "pins" of the Tabernacle which were of brass (significant of the flesh). It is used of something that can be removed, something that is not permanent. But in contrast it is also used symbolically of the things of God that cannot be removed.

In relation to Samson's hair being bound, reference is made to a "beam". The word only occurs twice in the Old Testament. The other occasion is in symbol for man's life that passes quickly without hope: "My days are swifter than a weaver's *shuttle*, and are spent without hope" (Job 7:6).

Again we see in the things that Samson suggests can make him weak, things that in themselves are unable to overcome the strength and power of the Almighty vested in him. They depict the life and strength of man who is destined to die without hope and who is powerless before the God who created him.

In all three tests we can see the lesson for Delilah and Israel, that all the things man uses to usurp the power and strength of God are in fact powerless against the Spirit of the Almighty, if a man has faith in Him.

The only way Samson's strength was overcome was when he allowed his faith to become weak and so failed to love his God with all his heart above all (and everyone) else – a time when Yahweh would no longer be with him.

Samson's weakness

Samson's weakness wasn't a carnal, fleshly lust for women. He took a wife of the Philistines to penetrate their defences and bring deliverance for his people in the purpose of God. He didn't go to a harlot's house for carnal satisfaction but lodged there, as did the two spies in the days of Joshua. He used his visit to bring judgement on Israel's enemy and their city of strength by possessing the gates of Gaza; something Israel should have done in possessing the land God had given to them.

He did love Delilah, an Israelite! But he was betrayed by her for the love of money. He allowed his love for her to overshadow his love for God. His weakness seems to be the manipulation of two women. He allowed his resistance to be broken down by their continual pleadings and trusted them with information he should have kept to himself. On the first occasion in chapter 14 the pleadings of his Philistine "wife" became part of God's providential hand in bringing judgement to one of the cities of the lords of the Philistines. It also led to the climax of events when Samson slew one thousand of the Philistines. The second, however, caused him to forsake, and compromise, the condition of his calling and separation to God, and therefore brought the loss of his eyes and ultimately his life. But even in that act God's final judgement on the cities of the Philistines through Samson was brought about. Through Samson's weakness and its consequences, Yahweh was to display His power one last time through His strong man of Israel.

Samson and the prophecy of Micah

In relation to Samson's confession to Delilah, compare these words in Micah 7:5: "Trust ye not in a friend, put ye not confidence in a guide: keep the doors of thy mouth from her that lieth in thy bosom".

Compare also the whole of this section of God's prophecy of Micah with Samson as a man of faith:

> "Trust ye not in a friend, put ye not confidence in a guide: keep the doors of thy mouth from her that lieth in thy bosom. For the son dishonoureth the father, the daughter riseth up against her mother, the daughter in law against her mother in law; a man's enemies are the men of his own house. *Therefore I will look unto the* LORD; *I will wait for the God of my salvation: my God will hear me. Rejoice not against me, O mine enemy: when I fall, I shall arise; when I sit in darkness, the* LORD *shall be a light unto me. I will bear the indignation of the* LORD, *because I have sinned against him, until he plead my cause, and execute judgment for me: he will bring me forth to the light, and I shall behold his righteousness.*[3] Then she that is mine enemy shall see it, and shame shall cover her which said unto me, Where is the LORD thy God? mine eyes shall behold her: now shall she be trodden down as the mire of the streets."   (7:5-10)

3   Cf. Hebrews 11:39,40.

This portion of Micah's prophecy has its basis in the days of Hezekiah when Jerusalem was being surrounded by the Assyrians and Sennacherib's officials were mocking Hezekiah and the people's faith in the Lord their God. Hezekiah himself was sick and the political state of Judah and society itself was in turmoil.

But this prophecy is also Messianic because it is quoted by the Lord and applied to himself and discipleship (Matthew 10:35-37). We can see in God's word through Micah allusions back to Samson and forward to Christ. Micah 7:1 is similar in language to the Lord's words in Matthew 21:19 and Luke 13:6-9. Micah 7:2 also has its counterpart in the way the Jews sought to slay the Lord during his ministry. In verses 7-9 we see echoes of Samson in the prison house and in Dagon's temple at his death. He looked to the Almighty using God's covenant name; not with his natural sight, as this had been erased by his enemies: but with the eye of faith. He looked beyond death to the light of the morning of resurrection when he would behold God's righteousness. So too would the Lord Jesus Christ of whom Samson was a type.

Compare also Micah 7:18-20 which surely echoes the faith Samson had in God's mercy and grace and the covenants of promise He had made to the fathers:

"Who is a God like unto thee, that pardoneth iniquity, and passeth by the transgression of the remnant of his heritage? he retaineth not his anger for ever, because he delighteth in mercy. He will turn again, he will have compassion upon us; he will subdue our iniquities; and thou wilt cast all their sins into the depths of the sea. Thou wilt perform the truth to Jacob, and the mercy to Abraham, which thou hast sworn unto our fathers from the days of old."

The other interesting link with this prophecy and Samson relates to Hezekiah's name. His name means 'the strength of Yah' – the very thing Samson was until his fall.

Samson's capture

Sadly, because of the pleadings of Delilah Samson lost sight of God's purpose with him. He failed to see the danger that her entreaties would bring:

> "And she said unto him, How canst thou say, I love thee, *when thine heart is not with me*? thou hast mocked me these three times, and hast not told me wherein thy great strength lieth. And it came to pass, when she pressed[4] him daily with her words, and urged him, so that his soul was vexed unto death."
> (Judges 16:15,16)

The result of Delilah's persistent pleadings was his confession to her recorded in verse 17:

> "... he told her *all his heart*, and said unto her, There hath not come a razor upon mine head; for I have been a Nazarite [*nâziyr*, one separated] unto God from my mother's womb: if I be shaven, then my strength will go from me, and I shall become weak, and be like any other man."

This information about his strength relating to his uncut hair must have been revealed to him by God as it was not part of the angelic message in chapter 13. This confession is surely the declaration of a man who, for almost forty years had remained faithful to God's purpose with him. He had been 'a separate one' to the Lord: initially through his parents' care and then through his own faithfulness to his calling. But now Samson tells Delilah *all his heart*: a heart that up until then had loved the Lord his God. Now it would seem he was prepared to put his love for Delilah above his love for Yahweh his God. Samson it seems is blind to the danger this revelation to Delilah was to bring about. He too fails the test of faith and love.

On this fourth occasion Samson allows Delilah to lull him into sleep on her knees. The word "sleep" means: 'to be slack or languid, i.e., (by implication) sleep (figuratively, to die)'. What

---

4   Strong: 'to compress, i.e., (figuratively) oppress, distress'. It is the same word as "lay sore" (Judges 14:17).

caused Samson to sleep in such a way as to be unaware of what was to happen while he slept we are not told. But for Samson this was to be a sleep of death for at that time he died spiritually (verse 19). This time the weakness of the flesh had become his downfall. The seven locks of his long hair were only an outward symbol of his separation to the Lord and the power God gave him through the Spirit ("seven" no doubt signifying the perfection of the strength God gave him). The physical cutting of his hair was the outward sign of him breaking his separation to God and so his strength "went" from him, and the Lord "departed" from him (verses 19,20). These two words are the same in Hebrew. They are identical to the phrase in verse 17, "will go".

As an aside, it is worth noting that this is the only time the record says the Lord departed from Samson in relation to his special position before Him. Again this poses the question: If Samson was meant to be a 'Nazarite' in the sense of Numbers 6, why didn't the Lord depart from him when he slew the lion or the many Philistines that were slain by his hand and brought him into contact with dead bodies? On these occasions the reverse happened: we are told the Spirit of the Lord *came upon him*.

Sadly now that was not to be the case. Samson awoke and presumed the Lord would be with him as before. He thought he would be able to go out and "shake"[5] himself as he had done previously. He believed the source of his strength was in the God he served and who had raised him up to be a deliverer. But he had departed from Him and so Yahweh had departed from Samson.

Samson was "afflicted" or humbled by Delilah when the locks of his hair were cut off. He had given his heart to her instead of staying faithful with all his heart to the Lord. Notice it says Delilah afflicted him. This wasn't meant to be her part in the bargain with the lords of the Philistines. She had been given a bribe to entice Samson so the Philistines could "bind him" and "afflict him" (verse 5). But once she had become part of their

---

5   The root meaning of this word is to growl and rustle the mane like a lion.

evil plans she too took pleasure in afflicting God's strong man of Israel.

Samson failed to remember, and hearken to, the words of the Lord in Deuteronomy 6:

> "Hear, O Israel: The LORD our God is one LORD: and thou shalt love the LORD thy God with all thine heart, and with all thy soul, and with all thy might."   (verses 4,5)

His heart was given to another, and as a result his soul was vexed. Up to now the Lord had been with him and His Spirit had given him the strength to do the Lord's work. But now the might (strength)[6] the Almighty had given him from time to time in the past was no longer there. He had allowed himself to depart from God, and He in turn departed from him. The special relationship Samson had with the Lord was severed. He was no longer God's *nâziyr* – His separated one.

David fell into a similar trap through his love of Bathsheba. Both had to face the consequences. Samson had failed to remember the words of Joshua to Israel before his death:

> "One man of you shall chase a thousand: for the LORD your God, he it is that fighteth for you, as he hath promised you. *Take good heed therefore unto yourselves, that ye love the LORD your God.*"   (Joshua 23:10,11)

Up to that moment in time the Lord had fulfilled His promise. He had fought for Israel through His Spirit coming upon Samson. Samson had literally fulfilled the words of Joshua: he had chased a thousand and slain them. But now he had failed to "take good heed" unto himself. This was the very thing Israel had failed to do all through the book of Judges, and would fail to do again in their later history. And so in revealing the secret of his strength to Delilah, and in this act alone, Samson becomes a type of his own people Israel. They too had departed from Yahweh and He had given them into the hands of their enemies just as now he was doing with Samson. But as we shall see, God's purpose with

---

6   This is a different word from the one in Deuteronomy 6:5.

Samson was not yet complete. His greatest act, as God's provided saviour, was yet to take place. The Lord's grace and mercy, and His response to faithful prayer, were to be shown dramatically as the life of Samson – the man of faith – comes to an end. But more than that, as we have emphasised, Samson's name is written in that list of men and women of faith who will, in God's good time, inherit the eternal promises made to the fathers of old.

Love the Lord

These events relating to Samson and Delilah leave us with the important lesson that we must love our Heavenly Father, and His Son, above our love for anyone, or anything, else. The words of the Lord spoken through Moses to Israel in Deuteronomy 6:4-9 are as important for us as the Lord Jesus taught (Matthew 22:37). Remember also some other words of the Lord in Matthew 10:37:

> "He that loveth father or mother more than me is not worthy of me: and he that loveth son or daughter more than me is not worthy of me."   (verse 37)

We must be sure to guard our separation as God's holy chosen people and not allow the things of the flesh or the temptations from others to deceive us and infiltrate our promise to serve Him and His Son. We must not compromise our faith, or play fast and loose with the things of God. If we do, we shall lose our spiritual sight, our faith and our spiritual strength.

Neither should we be like Delilah who was tempted with the love of money. We "cannot serve God and mammon" (Matthew 6:24). "The love of money is the root of all evil" (1 Timothy 6:10) and through it many have erred from the things of God as she did.

We need also to remember to learn from our mistakes, and in humility and contrition look once more to our Heavenly Father for forgiveness and help to overcome the consequences of our sins.

Spiritual sight

Samson, through the persistence of Delilah, had failed to keep the words of Deuteronomy 6:4,5 before the frontlets of his eyes. And so as a result of losing his spiritual sight he was to lose his natural sight as the Philistines bored out his eyes. But out of that weakness he was made strong again (Hebrews 11:34). Through God's mercy, and his faith (spiritual sight), he was to overcome his enemy on an even greater scale than he had during all his life of faith as God's given saviour. We shall consider this in the following chapter (page 121).

Finally, as we reflect on this incident of Samson and Delilah we ought to remember the vital lesson which the Apostle Paul clearly taught in 2 Corinthians 4:16-18. Spiritual sight outweighs human sight. We must look to the eternal not the temporal. Our spiritual eyesight is more important than our natural. We must look beyond the present to the future glory promised to us. Like Samson we may suffer in differing ways in our individual lives. But whatever our experiences we should remember the words of the inspired Apostle Paul that "the sufferings of this present time are not worthy to be compared with the glory which shall be revealed in us" (Romans 8:18).

9 |

Faith and strength out of weakness

The Philistine boast and mocking of Samson

THE Philistines, having captured Samson and bored out his eyes, took him back to Gaza, the very city of strength he had humiliated by taking the doors, posts and bar of their gate to Hebron (Judges 16:21).

There he was "bound" (to yoke or hitch) with fetters of brass and made to grind in the "prison house".[1] Brass in scripture has long been regarded as symbolic of the flesh. Samson's love of Delilah, more than his love of God, had been the result of letting the flesh have the upper hand. Now in a literal way he is bound by the flesh. He has no natural strength to break free.

So he is made to grind in the prison house. The Hebrew word for "grind" refers to grinding meal, something a woman or concubine would do. Samson was therefore made to act like a weaker vessel, no longer the strong man who had slain their warriors. Now it was his own strength that turned the mill wheel not the strength of the Lord. But maybe they humiliated him in this way to make up for the time, some twenty years earlier, when he had prevented them from grinding at the mill by burning their wheat fields. No doubt Samson too would reflect on the contrast between that time, when he had done so much damage to their economy as part of God's "occasion" against the Philistines, and his present situation.

---

1   "Prison" is the same Hebrew word for "bound".

Notice though what the record is then quick to tell us in Judges 16:22: "Howbeit the hair of his head began to grow again after he was shaven." While still alive and with his hair growing, which he could feel with his hands, there was a new opportunity for Samson to rededicate himself once again to being *separate* to his God and to finish the work He had raised him up to do. His growing hair would remind him of his separation to the Lord and the purpose He had for him. His uncut hair wasn't the source of his strength but had been the symbol of his special relationship with his God. Surely now, as he realised it was growing again, he would turn over in his mind all he had learned from his parents concerning God's purpose with him. He would reflect on all he had accomplished against his people's enemy in beginning their deliverance and the circumstances that had brought out his humiliation at the hands of a wicked woman he had chosen to love and confide in. We can only try and imagine the intense suffering Samson had gone through at the time his eyes were bored out and while he was bound, taken to Gaza and then imprisoned. What thoughts entered his mind, what questions he must have asked, we can again only contemplate; but we feel sure there must have been many prayers of repentance that Samson made to the Almighty during the long weeks and months of his imprisonment, which are not recorded. As a man of faith, yet still a man who was afflicted as all men are by the flesh, he would have asked: Why? After all he had done as God's saviour why had it come to this? But God was a God of salvation, a God of mercy and grace, as he himself believed, and as Micah later prophesied and which we have already seen echoes the experiences of God's strong man of Israel.

On a chosen day the lords of the Philistines gathered together, with the people, to boast and rejoice at the capture of Samson and to worship their god, Dagon (Judges 16:23,24).

"Our god hath delivered (given) into our hands (Samson) our enemy, and the destroyer of our country, which slew many of us."   (Judges 16:24)

Note once more what Samson was in their eyes:

- their enemy;
- the destroyer of their country;
- the one who slew many of them.

These three descriptions of Samson fit perfectly the record Judges gives us of Samson's dealings with the Philistines. He was the enemy who had possessed the gates of their 'strong' city, Gaza. He had destroyed their country, their economy, when he had brought fiery judgement on them as part of God's "occasion against the Philistines". He was also the one who had slain thirty men to obtain spoil; but also many with a great slaughter and a thousand more with the jawbone of an ass.

The Philistine boast that their god Dagon had given Samson into their hand was in fact a direct challenge to the God of Israel. Only He had the power to do that because their god was powerless as they were soon to discover once again. The Lord had delivered Samson into their hands when He departed, for a time, from His appointed saviour. Like Delilah, Samson had failed the test of faith and love.

Having boasted of his capture, and celebrated to the point of making their hearts merry, they called for Samson out of the prison house and set him between the pillars of the house, or temple, in order to make "sport" of him (verses 25,26). The word "sport" means, 'to laugh (in pleasure or detraction); by implication, to play'. The second occurrence in verse 25 is a different word in the Hebrew but has a similar meaning: i.e., 'to laugh outright (in merriment or scorn); by implication, to sport'. This second word is the one used of the children of Israel in Exodus 32:6 when they worshipped the golden calf during Moses' absence up Mount Horeb.

Samson was then led out by a lad and he asked to feel the pillars on which the house stood. Along with all the lords of the Philistines, the roof of the house contained some three thousand Philistines, all wishing to laugh at, and mock, the once strong man of Israel, their enemy (verse 27). But now Samson, once again, in faith, turns to his God. It wasn't enough that his hair had grown: that was only an outward sign. The strength, due to the Spirit of the Lord upon him, which he had lost by sin and the weakness of the flesh, he now sought to regain by humble and sincere prayer (verse 28).

Samson's final prayer

Samson, in this final prayer, calls unto the Lord using three of God's names, or titles:

"And Samson called unto the LORD, and said, O *Lord GOD*, remember me, I pray thee, and strengthen me, I pray thee, only this once, O *God*, that I may be at once avenged of the Philistines for my two eyes." (verse 28)

- "Lord" – Adonai – 'sovereign, ruler'.
- "GOD" – Yehohvih (equivalent to Yahweh – 'I am who I am / I will be who I will be') – the Covenant and Memorial name – the name that reveals God's purpose and glory.
- "God" – Elohim – 'mighty ones'.

This is Samson's God, the Sovereign Lord, the Covenant God; the One who is mighty ones.

Samson calls upon the Lord to:

"*Remember me, I pray thee.*" Remembrance is associated with the Covenant name of God – Yahweh – that was given to Moses (Exodus 3:14-17; 6:2-8).

"*Strengthen me, I pray thee.*" This associates with Elohim – the mighty ones – the angels who excel in strength; the spirit beings who encamp around those who fear God and deliver them (Psalm 34:7; 103:20).

"*Only this once.*" This is an appeal to the Sovereign Lord – Adonai – to exercise His will and once again cause His Spirit to come upon His servant, so Samson could be avenged of the loss of his eyes and complete the work God had given him to do.

Note also that his words "strengthen me, I pray thee, only this once, O God, that I may be at once avenged of the Philistines for my two eyes"[2] surely imply that Samson knew, and believed, that throughout his work for God, He had been the source of his strength. It was only when the Spirit of the Lord came upon him that he could achieve the great feats recorded of him. These displays of strength were not the actions of a man running wild and using his own natural power and inclinations or misusing the strength he received from God; but those of a man of faith, doing the will of Him who separated and empowered him by His Spirit to be a saviour of His people.

Use of the title – Lord GOD

Apart from its use in the Psalms and Prophetic writings, the following are the only other occurrences in the historical narrative of the use of the title "Lord GOD" – *Adonai Yehohvih*:

- Abraham twice (Genesis 15:2,8);
- Moses twice (Deuteronomy 3:24; 9:26);
- Joshua once (Joshua 7:7);
- Gideon once (Judges 6:22);
- *Samson* once (Judges 16:28);
- David six times (2 Samuel 7:18,19(×2),20,28,29);
- Solomon twice (1 Kings 2:26; 8:53).

The power of prayer

This final incident in Samson's life teaches us that we must always remember the importance, and power, of prayer, and who our Heavenly Father is. There are so many examples in scripture of men and women who offered prayers to the Almighty and were heard. The greatest example being *the* Saviour himself as we read in Hebrews 5:

---

2   There are a few variations of these words when you compare other translations. For example, cf. Rotherham, YLT and the RSV.

"Who in the days of his flesh, when he had offered up prayers and supplications with strong crying and tears unto him that was able to save him from death, and was heard in that he feared; though he were a Son, yet learned he obedience by the things which he suffered; and being made perfect, he became the author of eternal salvation unto all them that obey him."
(verses 7-9)

Our prayers, like the Lord's, are not to be self-based, but God-based, praying according to His will. We need, as the Lord Jesus taught, to focus on the Almighty and His purpose, seeking first His kingdom and righteousness, and then on our own requests (Matthew 6:9-13,24-34). The exhortation of scripture is to "pray without ceasing" (1 Thessalonians 5:17); "continuing instant in prayer" (Romans 12:12); "continue in prayer, and watch in the same with thanksgiving" (Colossians 4:2); "be careful for nothing; but in every thing by prayer and supplication with thanksgiving let your requests be made known unto God" (Philippians 4:6).

What a wonderful privilege this is to support and sustain us through all our days. Like Samson we too can call unto the Lord at any time, knowing He will always answer – but only according to His will.

A sincere and faithful man

The loss of his eyes was the permanent physical reminder to Samson of the temporary loss of his faith and commitment to the role he was born to fulfil.

If Samson had used his eyes in a lustful way throughout his life, as is often supposed, then would he have felt justified in asking Yahweh to avenge them? And would God have heard his prayer and once more strengthened him? But if, deep down, he was a man of faith, as the epistle to the Hebrews clearly tells us he was, but who made one drastic mistake: then surely he would have had the confidence to pray as he did, believing God would hear his prayer as a gracious and forgiving God. The avenging of his eyes was his way of completing the work Yahweh had strengthened him to do and he was prepared to die in the very act. It was his eye of faith and the honour of the God he served that he surely sought to be avenged for. His eyes had not been used for selfish lustful desires. Like the rest of his body and mind they had been used in service to his God. Surely the Lord would not have heard his prayer and strengthened him if it wasn't the prayer of *a sincere and faithful man*, who had been forgiven; a man who recognised his weakness and his failure: and who now sought once again to fulfil the will of God through him.

Later in the nation's history the good king Asa perhaps had Samson in mind (as well as the words of Jonathan and David) when he prayed to God in these words:

> "LORD, it is nothing with thee to help, whether with many, or with them that have no power: help us, O LORD our God; for we *rest* on thee, and in thy name we go against this multitude. O LORD, thou art our God; let not man prevail against thee."
> (2 Chronicles 14:11)

The Hebrew word for "rest" is the same as "lean" in Judges 16:26. Samson not only leant on the pillars, he rested on the Lord as did Asa. Sadly it was later in his reign when Asa failed once again to "rest" on Yahweh that he was punished for his lack of faith (2 Chronicles 16:7-12). The same encouragement to lean upon the Lord is found in the book of Proverbs:

> "Trust in the LORD with all thine heart; and *lean* not unto thine own understanding."   (Proverbs 3:5)[3]

Note also the word "power" used by Asa is the same as is used of Samson's "strength" in Judges 16.

The strength of Samson

In fact the references to Samson's "strength" are only found in Judges 16. The Hebrew word is 'from an unused root meaning to be firm; vigour, literally (force, in a good or a bad sense)' and occurs *seven times*:

---

3   Cf. also Isaiah 10:20; 50:10; Micah 3:11.

- Verse 5 – The lords of the Philistines desire Delilah to find "wherein his great *strength* lieth".
- Verse 6 – Delilah pleads with Samson to tell her "wherein thy great *strength* lieth".
- Verse 9 – Samson escapes capture and "his *strength* was not known".
- Verse 15 – After three attempts Delilah says, "Thou hast mocked me ... and ... not told me wherein thy great *strength* lieth".
- Verse 17 – Samson finally tells Delilah his heart and reveals that "if I be shaven, then my *strength* will go from me".
- Verse 19 – Having been shaven Samson's "*strength* went from him".
- Verse 30 – After praying to God Samson "bowed himself with (all his) *might*" (same original word as strength) and dies slaying 3,000 Philistines – God's work for him is complete.

As an aside, it is interesting that the sixth time his strength is mentioned is when it went from him. In scripture, six is the number for man and seven is the number of completion: and in Samson's case his work of beginning to deliver Israel from the Philistines was completed (note that the Hebrew word only occurs in one other place, in Judges with reference to Gideon – 6:14).

There is no other man of which it is said the Spirit of the Lord came upon him more than it is said of Samson. This was the source of Samson's strength which enabled him to do what he did as God's saviour, and again this surely emphasises his wonderful faith in the Lord his God, and that the Almighty was with him in his work for Him.

Samson's work is completed

Having prayed to his God, Samson took hold of the two middle pillars of the house, one with the right hand, the other with the left. There, with his arms stretched out, he cried out.

"And Samson said, Let me die with the Philistines. And he bowed himself with all his might; and the house fell upon the lords, and upon all the people that were therein. So the dead which he slew at his death were more than they which he slew in his life."   (Judges 16:30)

Why emphasise this fact if Samson was such a wayward character who God only recorded in His word because of the negative lessons we could learn from him? Why also emphasise this fact if he was meant to be a true 'Nazarite' as recorded in Numbers 6? Surely the reason we are being told this is that we have an illustration of how faith in the Almighty can overcome the flesh when God answers prayer and sends His angelic ministers to be with those who seek to serve Him faithfully. So Samson died in faith having received not the promise, God having provided some better thing for us, that he without us should not be made perfect.

The Philistines had made "sport" of Samson. They had laughed at him and had him in derision. But it is the Almighty who had the last 'laugh', as it will also be in the case of His purpose with the greater saviour – the Lord Jesus Christ. The same Hebrew word used of Samson being made "sport" by the Philistines in Judges 16:25,27 is used in Psalm 2:4 when the Lord shall "laugh" and have the heathen in derision. They had risen up against Him and His Anointed, but it was all according to God's predetermined purpose which would eventually see His Only begotten Son established as King on His holy hill of Zion; the one who as the seed of Abraham would possess the gate of his enemies.

"Ask of me, and I shall give thee the heathen for thine inheritance, and the uttermost parts of the earth for thy possession."   (Psalm 2:8)

So the Lord showed, through the power invested in Samson, who is the True and Only God. Dagon and his worshippers are destroyed, and in the Philistine city of strength Gaza, Samson, God's strong man of Israel, triumphs once again. *Light overcomes darkness in more ways than one.* They had boasted that it was their god Dagon who had delivered Samson into their hands. But that was in fact a challenge to the God of Israel who had allowed His chosen saviour to be delivered up and humiliated before them according to His determinate purpose to deliver Israel from their enemy. Centuries later the Lord was to allow His only begotten Son to suffer a similar fate in order to provide a way of saving men and women from sin and death (Acts 2:23).

So we see that Samson, through the strength of God, in these two incidents in Judges 16 relating to the city of Gaza overcame not only the *political* symbol of the Philistine city of strength by taking its gate's doors and posts to Hebron, but also its *religious* symbol and place of worship when the image and temple of Dagon is destroyed along with those who worshipped it.

Here surely is a wonderful type of Christ's future work: a time when he will bring to nought the political and religious systems of men and in their place establish God's kingdom and temple centred in Jerusalem, which shall never be destroyed but will stand forever (Daniel 2:44,45). That work began when he, like Samson, died with outstretched arms as a perfect sacrifice and Saviour from sin and death.

A place of rest

Now, at the end of his life, we are told of Samson's brethren[4] and all the house of his father (Judges 16:31):

> "Then his brethren and all the house of his father came down, and took him, and brought him up, and buried him between Zorah and Eshtaol in the burying place of Manoah his father. And he judged Israel twenty years." (verse 31)

These words are significant if we accept Samson as a man blessed by God and separated for the Lord's work of deliverance through His chosen Saviour. Once again scripture seems to be focusing our minds on a man of faith not a wayward son of Adam.

4   Cf. Judges 14:3.

It would seem, as we suggested in chapter 1 (page 1), that at last his example of faith had been noted. They, in faith, entered the territory of the Philistines to retrieve his body[5] in order to bury him in the very place God had "moved" him to be His chosen deliverer, the one who had judged Israel for twenty years. Note too that he was buried "in the burying place of Manoah his father". Manoah's name as we saw at the commencement of our studies means 'rest'. So how appropriate that his son, who had fought hard in faith to begin to deliver his people as their saviour, should now be laid in a place of rest, awaiting the glorious day of resurrection at *the* Saviour's return when the final rest will take place (Hebrews 4:9-11).

And so Samson's work was complete. The Lord did answer his prayer. He was indeed remembered. *He died in faith and his name appears in the list of the faithful* (Hebrews 11:13,39,40). He now awaits the fulfilment of the promises: the time when the one, of whom Samson was a type, will return to the earth to complete the work of possessing the gate of his enemies, both political and religious, including death itself. At that time, and by God's grace, the Master will remember, and reward, all the faithful of the ages past, including Samson, with eternal life in the age to come.

May we too echo Samson's prayer and the prayer of the thief on the cross next to our Lord, when he said:

"Lord, *remember me* when thou comest into thy kingdom."
(Luke 23:42)

In the final chapter of our study (page 133) we shall look at Samson as a type of Christ and also remind ourselves that the record of his life is written for our learning.

---

5 This was no mean task as they would have to search through the rubble of Dagon's house, and the dead Philistine bodies strewn among it.

Types and lessons

Samson was a man of faith

OUR purpose in revisiting the record of the life of Samson, and comparing scripture with scripture, has been to defend Samson as a man of faith by prayerfully seeking to see what God's purpose with him really was. We certainly have not sought to harm the faith of any who hold, what we may call, the traditional view of Samson. However, since engaging in this study we have become aware of how many others also believe that Samson was an outstanding example of a man or woman of faith.

We have seen that there is evidence to support the view that he is not the wayward, lustful man with bulging muscles as is usually portrayed. We may not, as we stated in the first chapter, have found the answers to all the problems in the record of Samson's life, or provided a satisfactory alternative interpretation of the record in a number of cases; but we have tried to demonstrate that the inspired scripture record reveals that he was *a great man of faith*, who trusted the Lord his God based on the Almighty *separating* him to *begin* to deliver Israel from the Philistine domination, and based upon his own understanding of the covenants of promise.

God's Spirit came upon him: that gave him his strength. God's power worked through Samson to overcome the enemy. He looked upon himself as the Lord's servant and totally relied on Him. He was a *saviour* for his people: but like the Lord Jesus

Christ was rejected by them because of their lack of faith. Samson, with God's help, worked alone against the Philistines without Israel incurring the Philistines' wrath upon them. The Philistines regarded him as their enemy, the destroyer of their country who had slain many of them, and who they desired to capture and destroy. But like all men other than the Lord Jesus Christ, Samson did sin, and so faced the consequences.

Despite his one failing with regard to God's restriction upon him concerning his hair, Samson's faith remained strong; and again after his fall he put his trust in the Lord, even to his death. He was alone in his work for God – a shining light in a dark apathetic age when the majority around him had turned from the Lord to other gods, failed to fulfil His word, and had submitted to their enemy without opposition.

Even though his physical light was put out, Samson saw the light of God's glory and grace, and His purpose with him, through his spiritual sight. He showed his people, if only they had followed his example and loved the Lord, *that one man with God is a majority* and that the consequences of sin can be overcome.

Just as he learned from the faith and example of others who trusted in God's strength, so he also has left a powerful example for all men and women of faith down the ages. He is part of the great cloud of witnesses that we must learn from in Hebrews 11.

"Wherefore seeing we also are compassed about with *so great a cloud of witnesses*, let us lay aside every weight, and the sin which doth so easily beset us, and let us run with patience the race that is set before us ..."   (Hebrews 12:1)

Samson ran his race and died in faith not having received the promises; but awaits the day, in God's grace, when we shall be made perfect with him at our Lord's return.

"And these all [including Samson], having obtained a good report through faith, received not the promise: God having provided some better thing for us, that they without us should not be made perfect."   (11:39,40)

Before we conclude our studies of Samson let us consider a number of comparisons between him and some New Testament characters.

Samson and Paul

Consider these words of the Apostle Paul in relation to the life of Samson:

> "But I beseech you, that I may not be bold when I am present with that confidence, wherewith I think to be bold against some, which think of us as if we walked according to the flesh. For though we walk in the flesh, we do not war after the flesh: (For the weapons of our warfare *are not carnal, but mighty through God* to the pulling down of strong holds;) casting down imaginations, and every high thing that exalteth itself against the knowledge of God, and bringing into captivity every thought to the obedience of Christ; and having in a readiness to revenge all disobedience, when your obedience is fulfilled."   (2 Corinthians 10:2-6)

Remember that Paul, like Samson, was separated from his mother's womb for the purpose the Lord had with him (cf. Galatians 1:15; Romans 1:1). The Apostle to the Gentiles knew where his strength lay as he went forth doing the work he was called to do. He had to learn that, "My grace is sufficient for thee: for my strength is made perfect in weakness" (2 Corinthians 12:9).

If we reflect on these words of Paul we can see echoes from the record of Samson as a man of faith. His life and weapons were not based on carnal things but were mighty through the Spirit of God coming upon him. He too, literally pulled down strong holds when he pulled down the Philistine city of Gaza's gate and doors – the city whose name means 'strong, or strength'. He also cast down the temple of Dagon and the people who had exalted their god above the true God – the God of Israel.

What Samson did literally we have to do spiritually. As we have already reminded ourselves, our strength and trust must be in our Heavenly Father and His Son.

Samson and John Baptist

Note also some parallels between Samson and John Baptist.

- Both were born to barren women by the direct intervention of God (Luke 1:7-13).
- Both were separated by God to begin a work, but were only given one aspect of the 'Nazarite vow' to keep. In both cases this was not voluntary (Luke 1:15).
- Both lived in the wilderness at times (Luke 1:80).
- Both were strengthened by the Spirit (Luke 1:15).
- Both died as a result of a wicked woman (Mark 6:16-28).
- Both did work that was completed by those who came after them.
  - Samson prepares the way for Samuel and David to complete the work.
  - John prepared the way for the Lord Jesus and his apostles (Matthew 3:1-12).

Samson as a type of Christ

When we come to consider Samson and the Lord Jesus Christ there are so many ways in which Samson's birth, life and death can be seen as a type, or at least share common characteristics, with events in the life of our Lord and Saviour. This is more readily seen if we regard Samson as a man of faith rather than a man who was constantly falling short of his calling. The following is a list of the most outstanding ways in which his life portrayed that of the coming, promised, Messiah who was to be God's ultimate Saviour. This list is not meant to be exhaustive.

- Both births were announced by an angel to a woman (Luke 1:31).
- Both were made of a woman, made under the law (Galatians 4:4).
- Both births were miraculous (Luke 1:27).

- Both were born at a time of domination by their enemies (Luke 3:1).

- Both were separated (set apart) to God from birth (Luke 1:35; Acts 4:27).

- Both were born to be Saviours of their people (Matthew 1:21).

- Both had a name associated with the sun (of righteousness) (Malachi 4:2).

- Both shone as lights in a dark age (John 8:12).

- Both grew and were blessed by God (Luke 2:40,52).

- Both received the Spirit of God (Matthew 3:16).

- Both were made strong by God (Psalm 80:17).

- Both went into enemy territory to overcome it (Hebrews 2:9,14).

- Both had parents who didn't understand the work they were doing (Luke 2:49).

- Both told a riddle or parable (Matthew 13, etc.).

- Both were born to be Judges (Isaiah 9:6,7; John 5:22,27).

- Both were rejected by their people who accepted others as their rulers (John 19:15).

- Both allowed themselves to be taken and led to the enemy (Matthew 26:53; Isaiah 53:7).

- Both were thirsty after a battle with the enemy (John 19:28).

- Both were the Lord's servants (Philippians 2:7; Isaiah 42:1; Matthew 20:28; Luke 22:27).

- Both possessed the gate of their enemies and took the government on their shoulders (Genesis 22:17; Isaiah 9:6,7; cf. Psalm 2:8,9; 1 Corinthians 15:16).

- Both lived lives dedicated to serving God (Luke 22:42; John 6:38; Matthew 4:10).

- Both had their souls vexed unto death and were afflicted (John 12:27; Isaiah 53:4,7).
- Both knew they would be betrayed (Luke 22:21,22).
- Both were betrayed for silver and by friendship (cf. the number thirty: Matthew 26:14-16; 26:50).
- Both were delivered to the Gentiles (Matthew 27:1,2).
- Both were blinded / blindfolded (Luke 22:64).
- Both were taken from a prison house (Isaiah 53:8).
- Both were mocked before death (Matthew 27:31).
- Both bowed themselves before death (John 19:30).
- Both displayed their greatest faith shortly before death (Luke 22:42; 23:46).
- Both prayed to God before their death and were heard (Hebrews 5:7).
- Both made a once for all sacrifice (Hebrews 10:10).
- Both accomplished their greatest victory in death (Hebrews 2:14).
- Both destroyed their enemy in death (Hebrews 2:14; 9:26).
- Both were taken by friends and family to be buried (Matthew 27:57-61).
- Both are listed in the 'hall of faith' in the epistle to the Hebrews, Jesus being the greatest example of all (Hebrews 12:2).

Lessons from the record of Samson

The record of Samson's life teaches us many lessons, both positive and negative, which we have already considered throughout these studies. We must remember that all inspired scripture is written for our learning.[1] Hopefully, from our study of Samson, we have seen that there are more positive lessons than negative ones to learn from the life of this man of God.

---

1   Cf. Romans 15:4.

He was provided as a Saviour at a time when Israel did evil in God's sight. Unlike other times in the period of the Judges the people had not cried unto the Lord. Despite this, God showed the wonder of His mercy and grace in providing a way of salvation in the son born to Manoah and his wife. In the same way Paul writes in his epistle to the Romans that it was when "we were yet sinners Christ died for us" (Romans 5:8). Here we see the grace of God at work again.

"God so loved the world, that he gave his only begotten Son, that whosoever believeth in him should not perish, but have everlasting life."   (John 3:16)

Like Israel of old, naturally, we are undeserving of God's grace and love, but we must thank Him daily for the provision He has made for our salvation.

Samson lived at a time when "every man did that which was right in his own eyes" (Judges 21:25). We have seen from the record that, although this has also been the opinion of Samson by many commentators, there is another way of understanding the events recorded of him. Although he appears to be doing things against God's law, he was in fact doing those things as part of God's purpose with him. So too the one who was the antitype of Samson, the Lord Jesus Christ. To those around him, especially the religious leaders of the day, the Lord was breaking God's laws. But we know that just as the Spirit of God was upon Samson, it had come upon the Lord, and so all he did was according to God's purpose with him. That Spirit power was used to do good: even on the Sabbath Day. But unlike Samson who did sin and fall short of his calling, our Lord Jesus Christ was faithful and obedient even to death upon the cross, leaving us the perfect example to follow.

Conclusion

We feel sure we have not exhausted the lessons we can learn from the life of Samson, and the links we can find with other scriptures, but we have hopefully seen the positive, rather than negative, scripture teaching concerning him.

In all these things the Lord Jesus Christ is our perfect example to follow. He is our God-given Saviour who at his first advent began his work of deliverance which he will complete in us by God's grace, when he comes again to subdue all his enemies; the last enemy to be destroyed is death (1 Corinthians 15:26). He is the greatest example of faith and we must look to him as the author and finisher of faith as we seek to lay aside every weight and the sin which does so easily beset us (Hebrews 12:1-3).

Unlike Samson and the Lord Jesus Christ we do not have the direct working of the Spirit of God in our lives. Instead we have God's Spirit word that can make us wise to salvation through faith in His Son. The inspired scriptures of old were written for our learning. They contain so many examples, or types, for us to heed as we, like the faithful of old, strive to overcome – and not fulfil the lust of the flesh. Instead we must walk in the Spirit, developing its fruit in our lives of service to our Heavenly Father and our fellowship the one with the other (Galatians 5:16-26).

We also have the promise that as we seek to serve the Lord, in fear, His angels will encamp around us and deliver us (Psalm 34:7). The message of this Psalm is not that believing, trusting and fearing God is a kind of assurance policy that prevents us from experiencing the trials and troubles of life, or even a tragic death. Rather it is saying that despite experiencing these things, as Samson and the Lord Jesus did along with other faithful men and women of old,[2] we shall be finally redeemed out of them. For some that deliverance will occur during their lifetime, but for all it will ultimately be, by God's grace, a deliverance out of death that we may be blessed with eternal life in the age to come.

So then let us learn the lessons that are there in scripture from Samson's life. But more than that, let us look forward, in hope, to the day of our Lord's return, when the greater than Samson will be victorious over the power of sin forever.

---

2   Cf. Hebrews 11:33-38.

"... thanks be to God, which giveth us the victory through our Lord Jesus Christ. Therefore, my beloved brethren, be ye stedfast, unmoveable, always abounding in the work of the Lord, forasmuch as ye know that your labour is not in vain in the Lord."   (1 Corinthians 15:57,58)

Finally, let us remember once more the words at the conclusion of Hebrews 11 concerning the faithful of old – including Samson:

"And these all, having obtained a good report through faith, received not the promise: God having provided some better thing for us, that they without us should not be made perfect."
(Hebrews 11:39,40)

Scripture index